# McCheyne's
# DUNDEE

# McCheyne's
# DUNDEE

Bruce McLennan

**Reformation Heritage Books**
Grand Rapids, Michigan

*McCheyne's Dundee*
© 2018 by Bruce McLennan

**Reformation Heritage Books**
2965 Leonard St. NE
Grand Rapids, MI 49525
616–977–0889
orders@heritagebooks.org
www.heritagebooks.org

*Printed in the United States of America*
18 19 20 21 22 23/10 9 8 7 6 5 4 3 2 1

Library of Congress Cataloging-in-Publication Data

Names: McLennan, Bruce, author.
Title: McCheyne's Dundee / Bruce McLennan.
Description: Grand Rapids, Michigan : Reformation Heritage Books, 2018. |
   Includes bibliographical references.
Identifiers: LCCN 2017058510 (print) | LCCN 2017060655 (ebook) | ISBN
   9781601785916 (epub) | ISBN 9781601785909 (pbk. : alk. paper)
Subjects: LCSH: Church of Scotland. Presbytery of Dundee—History—19th
   century. | Dundee (Scotland)—Church history—19th century. | M'Cheyne,
   Robert Murray, 1813-1843. | Burns, William Chalmers, 1815-1868.
Classification: LCC BX9074.D79 (ebook) | LCC BX9074.D79 M35 2018
   (print) | DDC 285/.2412709034—dc23
LC record available at https://lccn.loc.gov/2017058510

*For additional Reformed literature, request a free book list from Reformation Heritage Books at the above regular or e-mail address.*

# Contents

# Acknowledgments

This work could not have been completed without the cooperation and assistance of staff of the following centers, whose help is greatly appreciated: Dundee City Archives; Dundee Central Public Library, Local History/Family History Department; National Library of Scotland, Edinburgh; New College Library, University of Edinburgh; the Evangelical Library, London.

I would especially like to express my thanks to the editor and staff of Reformation Heritage Books for all their guidance and help in the final presentation of this work.

# Introduction:
# Instruments of Spiritual Blessing

While Dundee was gradually establishing itself in the mid-nineteenth century as the third city of Scotland, with a rapidly expanding economy, it was the religious revival that began in the autumn of 1839 that drew the attention of observers throughout Scotland and beyond. Two names associated with the awakening in Dundee and the surrounding district are William Chalmers Burns (1815–1868) and Robert Murray McCheyne (1813–1843), in spite of the relatively short time they spent in that city. Burns spent only about seven months there from early April to late November 1839. (He did spend an additional four months as a temporary pastor in the Dudhope area of Dundee, beginning in December 1840.)[1] During 1839 he made two trips back to his father's charge in Kilsyth and saw God at work in revival there.

Although minister from November 1836 until his death in March 1843, McCheyne was often involved in the Lord's work outside Dundee for a variety of reasons. He was often away at Communion seasons—for example, at Newton-on-Ayr in Ayrshire, Auchtermuchty in Fife, and at Larbert or Kelso.[2] David Robertson comments that for much of 1840 he was "busy speaking at churches all over the

---

1. Tom Lennie, *Land of Many Revivals* (Fearn, Scotland: Christian Focus, 2015), 353.

2. McCheyne preached at Auchtermuchty August 5, 1841. Manuscript Notebooks and Letters of Robert Murray McCheyne, 1.12 (hereafter cited as MACCH); L. J. Van Valen, *Constrained by His Love* (Fearn, Scotland: Christian Focus, 2002), 365, 410; and Andrew A. Bonar, *Memoir and Remains of the Rev. Robert Murray McCheyne*, new ed. (Edinburgh: Oliphant, Anderson and Ferrier, 1892), 136.

country to crowded meetings on the subject of Jewish evangelism."[3] To illustrate this, McCheyne records in his diary a trip to Glasgow with Andrew Bonar of Collace on behalf of the Jews when he had been back in his parish only a few weeks after his Palestine trip, which had taken him and Bonar from Scotland for six months.[4] This also took him to the United Synod of Northern Ireland on two occasions, from July 7 to 25, 1840, and again in July 1841.[5] In 1840 he exchanged pulpits for a month with Bonar while their *Narrative of a Mission of Inquiry to the Jews* was being written up.[6] Midweek services elsewhere, visits to London and the General Assembly to make a maiden speech in May 1840, together with many periods of illness meant that his time in Dundee would have been less than five years rather than about six and a half.[7] It is no wonder that his congregation "began to murmur at his absence."[8]

From their student days, both Burns and McCheyne had strong interests in the mission field abroad. There is a retrospective note in Burns's diary in which his missionary interest is revealed:

> At Glasgow University, during the winter of 1837–8, I was led, from my connection with the college missionary association, to feel so deeply my personal responsibility in regard to the spread of the gospel among the heathen, that after much prayer and many exercises of soul, I took the solemn step of writing to my father, to request, if he thought good, he should communicate with Dr Gordon, the convenor of our

---

3. David Robertson, *Awakening: The Life and Ministry of Robert Murray McCheyne* (Fearn, Scotland: Christian Focus, 2010), 155–56. In a letter from McCheyne to his parents, dated April 24, 1841, he wrote, "In Ireland for Jewish mission work." MACCH 2.7.1.

4. Andrew A. Bonar, *Memoir*, 124.

5. Andrew A. Bonar, *Memoir*, 133; McCheyne to parents, April 24, 1841, MACCH 2.7.1.

6. Andrew A. Bonar, *Memoir*, 141. Bonar records, "Accordingly, during four or five weeks, he remained in Collace, my flock enjoying his Sabbath day services and his occasional visits, while he was set free from what would have been the never-ceasing interruptions of his own town."

7. He was ordained November 24, 1836, and called home March 25, 1843.

8. Andrew A. Bonar, *Memoir*, 145.

India committee, and let him know that, should the Church deem me qualified, I would be ready to go as a missionary to Hindustan.[9]

This fell through because the India committee did not like the idea of Burns going to St. John's, New Brunswick, at the request of the colonial committee, before going to India. Two months after Burns began his ministry at St. Peter's, the India committee asked Burns to go as a missionary to Poonah in Bombay, and the Jewish committee asked him to go to Aden in Arabia. Having begun his labors in Dundee, "that memorable field," service abroad had to wait. After being greatly used in evangelism in Scotland, England, Ireland, and Canada, he at last sailed as a missionary to China in 1847 for what was to be his life's work.[10]

Even before he attained his majority, McCheyne's missionary interests were developing. As his student days drew to a close, he often discussed and prayed with his close friend and prayer partner Alexander Somerville about whether God was calling them to missionary work or to serve as a minister at home. In his diary for June 4, 1832, he recorded, "Walking with A. Somerville by Craigleith, conversing on missions. If I am to go to the heathen to speak of the unsearchable riches of Christ, this one thing must be given me, to be out of the reach of the baneful influence of esteem or contempt. If worldly motives go with me, I shall never convert a soul, and shall lose my own in the labor."[11] McCheyne followed the labors of missionaries abroad with great interest. In particular, he was greatly impressed by the life of David Brainerd.[12] Bonar remarked of his friend that "to the last days of his life, his thoughts often turned to foreign lands."[13]

---

9. Andrew A. Bonar, *Memoir*, 145.

10. Michael D. McMullen, *God's Polished Arrow: William Chalmers Burns* (Fearn, Scotland: Christian Focus, 2002), 24; Islay Burns, *Memoir of the Rev. William Chalmers Burns* (London: James Nisbet, 1870), 56.

11. Andrew A. Bonar, *Memoir*, 17.

12. Andrew A. Bonar, *Memoir*, 20.

13. Andrew A. Bonar, *Memoir*, 28.

Although Burns appeared to be of a robust constitution, McCheyne, by contrast, suffered much ill health. While still at university in 1830, he first showed signs of weakness.[14] Bonar noted in his diary his concern that McCheyne was "already threatened with dangerous symptoms about his lungs."[15] McCheyne himself felt his weakness. On November 18, 1834, he composed one of his best-loved hymns, "Jehovah Tsidkenu," during a fever from which he was not sure he would recover. He really felt himself to be "treading the valley, the shadow of death."[16] Even his trip to Palestine did not seem to make much difference to his constitution. Burns met him on his return to Dundee and commented, "He seems in but weak health, and not very sanguine about ever resuming the full duties of a parish minister. O Lord, spare thy servant, if it be for the glory of thy name, and restore his full strength that he may yet be the means of winning many souls for Jesus. Amen."[17] In his biography, Robertson has given more consideration to McCheyne's condition than others, suggesting he not only suffered from depression, which his brother David had also had, but questions if he could be called a "workaholic."[18] Certainly, as chapter 3 will reveal, he was a tireless worker.

The above factors might suggest that Burns and McCheyne would not make any great impact on Dundee: the short amount of time they spent there, their missionary interests, their relative youthfulness and inexperience—in Burns's case as a largely untried and untested licentiate. Added to this was McCheyne's ongoing bodily weakness. Nevertheless, both these men proved to be, in the providence of God, instruments of great spiritual blessing to the people of Dundee and beyond, linking their names forever with those times of refreshing in the late 1830s and early 1840s. It is necessary first, however, to set the scene by considering something of the social and economic conditions of the town in which they labored.

---

14. Robertson, *Awakening*, 67.
15. Robertson, *Awakening*, 67.
16. Andrew A. Bonar, *Memoir*, 62–63; Robertson, *Awakening*, 68.
17. Islay Burns, *Memoir*, 130; McMullen, *God's Polished Arrow*, 45.
18. Robertson, *Awakening*, 67–74 (chap. 6, "Oppression and Depression").

# 1

# Dundee in the 1830s and 1840s

In population, manufactures, and trade; in the luxury and comfort which prevail, Dundee has perhaps advanced faster than any similar town in the kingdom. There are men alive in it who remember when its population was only one-fifth of what it is now; when its harbour was a crooked wall, often inclosing but a few fishing or smuggling craft; when its spinning-mills were things unknown and unthought of; and its trade hardly worthy of the name.

—*Dundee in 1793 and 1833: The First and Second Statistical Account*

The social consequences of the appearance of the swelling sea of new faces in the early decades of the Victorian era were profound. Plague had disappeared but only to be replaced by other killer diseases—some of which had made an appearance earlier—such as cholera (1832, 1849, 1853 and 1866), typhus (1837 and 1847), smallpox, measles, whooping cough and scarlet fever. Typhus lingered on in Dundee.... The spread of these had much to do with chronic overcrowding, notably in the vicinity of the mills and factories.... In large part the squalor...was associated with cramped living conditions, as property was further and further sub-divided to house the incomers. The existing housing stock, however, was insufficient to cope with such a massive influx of people. Few employers built houses for their workers.

—C. A. Whately, D. B. Swinfen, and A. M. Smith, *The Life and Times of Dundee*

One of the results of both the Agricultural and Industrial Revolutions was a major demographic shift, which led to a concentration of Scotland's population in towns and cities. Prior to this, the population of Scotland had been much more evenly distributed throughout the country. A survey conducted by Alexander Webster in 1755 revealed that 51 percent of Scotland's population lived in the Highlands, and only 37 percent in Central Scotland, which included Dundee. The government census of 1861 presented quite a different picture: the Highland population was reduced to 33 percent, while that of Central Scotland had risen to 58 percent.[1]

The growth of Dundee in the late eighteenth century had been gradual: 12,426 in 1766; 15,700 in 1781; and 19,329 in 1788. The 1833 statistical account for Dundee, however, revealed a more rapid growth: 26,804 in 1801; 29,616 in 1811; 30,575 in 1821; and 45,355 in 1831. This did not include the seafaring people, who might number 2,500, which would then give a total of 47,855.[2] This was to shoot up in the next decades to 79,000 in 1851, and then 90,000 in 1861.[3] With regard to the phenomenal growth that was taking place, in 1831 the *Dundee, Perth, and Cupar Advertiser* commented, "We are not aware that the population of any other town in the empire has increased with equal rapidity."[4] Ten years later, the population was 66,232, an increase of 20,877.[5] Dundee was on its way to becoming the third-largest city in Scotland, after Glasgow and Edinburgh.

---

1. James Grey Kyd, ed., *Scottish Population Statistics, Including Webster's Analysis of Population, 1755*, Scottish History Society, 3rd series, vol. 44 (Edinburgh: T. & A. Constable, 1952), xviii. For the purposes of Webster's survey, Central Scotland comprised the counties of Ayr, Dumbarton, Lanark, Renfrew, Clackmannan, Stirling, the Lothians, Fife, and Dundee City.

2. *Dundee in 1793 and 1833: The First and Second Statistical Accounts*, with an introduction by Annette M. Smith, facsimile ed. (St. Andrews: St. Andrews University Library, 1991), 17, 84.

3. S. G. E. Lythe and John Butt, *An Economic History of Scotland 1100–1939* (Glasgow and London: Blackie and Son, 1975), 245 (see esp. appendix 2, "Population of the Principal Towns").

4. *Dundee, Perth, and Cupar Advertiser*, July 21, 1831.

5. *Dundee, Perth, and Cupar Advertiser*, June 18, 1841.

Dundee's growth can be attributed to several causes. Some of those affected by the Highland Clearances and, from the 1840s on, by the Highland potato famine, made Dundee their home. There was a sufficient number for a Gaelic chapel to be erected in 1791, though only just over one percent of the town's population was Highland born.[6] Many came in from neighboring counties like Angus and Fife, either because they had been displaced by the gradual introduction of machinery on the farms or because they hoped to earn more than they had as poorly paid farm workers. Dundee was also developing one of the largest whaling fleets in Britain.[7] From 1810 on, the harbor commissioners supervised the enlarging of the Dundee docks. This enabled as many as 319 different sailing vessels to be registered and sail from Dundee. There was, therefore, a substantial seafaring community, which continued to grow for some time.

It was the linen trade in particular, however, that drew the population. While handloom weaving continued until midcentury, by 1832 there were more than thirty flax-spinning mills driven by steam engines.[8] Peter Carmichael (1809–1891), who rose to become manager of Baxter Brothers and engineer of some impressive industrial buildings, noted that the mills in the 1830s employed more than three thousand workers. Of these, more than a third were under eighteen, and about one-fifth were under fourteen years of age.[9] All in all, 6,828 families were employed in the different departments of the linen trade.[10] With this concentration on the one trade, Dundee "led Europe in its capture of the world's markets for machine-spun flax

---

6. *Dundee in 1793 and 1833*, 40; C. A. Whately, D. B. Swinfen, and A. M. Smith, *The Life and Times of Dundee* (Edinburgh: John Donald Publishers, 1993), 103. The 1851 census gives 809 as the figure for Highland-born residents.

7. Whately, Swinfen, and Smith, *Life and Times of Dundee*, 89–90.

8. Bruce Lenman, Charlotte Lythe, and Enid Gauldie, *Dundee and Its Textile Industry, 1850–1914*, Abertay Historical Society, no. 14 (Dundee, Scotland: n.p., 1969), 8.

9. Peter Carmichael Biographical Works, Dundee University Archive Room, MS 102/1, 177.

10. *Dundee in 1793 and 1833*, 91.

and the coarse linen cloth woven with it."[11] By the mid-1850s, however, jute had begun to overtake linen, and Dundee soon earned the reputation of being a "one-industry town."[12]

## Conditions of Employment in the Mills

There being no compulsory education until the 1870s, work began at a young age, though "the deepest horrors of child exploitation were gradually eliminated in the middle decades of the nineteenth century."[13] Evidence of these horrors was brought more and more to the attention of the government. In 1832 Dundee workers sent two petitions to Parliament. In one they protested the hours that young people between the ages of six and eighteen had to work, praying that the hours might be reduced. In the other they asked for a reduction to eleven and a half hours a day, or a sixty-six-hour week.[14] To petitions like this throughout the country was added the revelations of the parliamentary Royal Commission set up to investigate conditions in the factories. In 1833 Robert Arnot gave evidence to a parliamentary committee from his time as overseer at Baxter's Mill in Dundee. He described what he saw: "The boys, when too late of a morning, dragged naked from their beds by the overseers, and even by the master, with their clothes in their hands to the mill, where they put them on." This was done "oftener than he can tell, and the boys were strapped naked as they got out of bed." His testimony was confirmed by Barbara Watson, who worked at the same mill. She described similar treatment being meted out to the young girls.[15]

---

11. Louise Miskell, C. A. Whately, and Bob Harris, eds., *Victorian Dundee: Images and Realities* (Edinburgh: Tuckwell Press, 2000), 3.

12. Miskell, Whately, and Harris, *Victorian Dundee*, 2.

13. T. C. Smout, *A Century of the Scottish People, 1830–1930* (London: Fontana Press, 1977), 95.

14. Peter Carmichael Biographical Works, 178; Peter Carmichael, *The Dundee Textile Industry 1790–1885: From the Papers of Peter Carmichael of Arthurstone*, ed. Enid Gauldie, Scottish History Society, 4th series, vol. 6 (Edinburgh: Constable for the Scottish Historical Society, 1969), 51.

15. Parliamentary Papers 1833, vol. 20, A1, 40, quoted in E. Royston Pike,

Sir David Barry, a doctor appointed by the Royal Commission to report on Scotland, related the sad case of a worker who had entered the mill at the age of nineteen:

> Married. No children. Very hoarse. Aged twenty-five. Employed in carding room. Began mill-work about six years ago. Has felt her chest much oppressed about nine months ago: threw up a tea-cup full of dark blood with thick spittle this day at two-o'clock. Breathing much oppressed with wheezing, is really very ill. If any other employment presented, would leave the mill. Was brought up at country service. Obliged to sit up in bed at night from difficulty in breathing. Earns five shillings per week. Cannot write.[16]

Not only were conditions in the mills unhealthy, with temperatures being kept artificially high, but also the bosses were manipulating working hours. One local lad, James Myles, who described his early work experience at a spinning mill from seven years of age in a book that was not questioned or challenged at the time, had this to say with regard to hours of work: "In reality there were no regular hours, master and managers did with us as they liked. The clocks at the factories were often put forward in the morning and back at night, and instead of being instruments for the measurement of time, they were used as cloaks for cheatery and oppression."[17]

The Althorp Factory Act of 1833, in the light of evidence presented, stipulated that no child under nine years of age should be employed. Those aged nine to thirteen should work no more than nine hours a day. Those aged thirteen to eighteen years were limited to twelve hours a day. Factory inspectors were also appointed to see to enforcing the act. The hours of work were still long, however; a

---

*Human Documents of the Industrial Revolution in Britain* (London: Allen and Unwin, 1966), 150–51.

16. T. C. Smout, *A History of the Scottish People 1560–1830* (London: Fontana Press, 1972), 389.

17. James Myles, *Chapters in the Life of a Dundee Factory Boy: An Autobiography* (Dundee, Scotland: McCosh, Park and Dewars, 1850), 12–13.

maximum of fifty-four hours a week for those aged nine to thirteen, and seventy-two hours for those thirteen to eighteen. By the early 1830s, therefore, "it was overwhelmingly an industry [i.e., textile] employing adolescents rather than one employing young children."[18]

The day was still long, however, with only two half-hour breaks, one for breakfast, and the other for dinner. A six-day week was normal with only two days off in the year. Sunday would be regarded by many as a time to sleep and to recover strength for the next week's work.[19]

One of the unfortunate features of employment in the mills, from a family point of view, was that the owners, like Baxter or Cox, preferred to employ women and children at much less cost. Dundee was known as a women's city for at least two reasons: for one hundred years, women outnumbered men, and more women worked in Dundee than in any other town or city in Scotland.[20] Dundee was described as "a city where men were frequently dependent upon the earnings of mothers, sisters and daughters." Men were often reduced to doing the household chores in a role-reversal situation.[21]

Wages were not high. Flax dressers got from ten to twelve shillings weekly, girls and boys three to six shillings, women five to eight shillings, and weavers seven to ten shillings a week. In those days, twenty shillings made up one pound sterling, and rent could be as much as four pounds a week, consuming half a family's income. Yet these wagers were regarded as adequate to live on.[22]

18. Smout, *History of the Scottish People*, 389.

19. Smout, *History of the Scottish People*, 390.

20. Norman Watson, "Emerging from Obscurity: How Dundee Women Made Their Mark," in *Dundee: A Voyage of Discovery*, ed. Graham Ogilvy (Edinburgh: Mainstream, 1999), 199; A. M. Carstairs, "The Nature and Diversification of Employment in Dundee in the Twentieth Century," in *Dundee and District*, ed. S. J. Jones (Dundee, Scotland: Dundee Local Executive Committee of the British Association for the Advancement of Science, 1968), 321.

21. Whately, Swinfen, and Smith, *Life and Times of Dundee*, 114.

22. Carmichael, *Dundee Textile Industry*, 52.

## Inadequate Housing for the Growing Population

While working conditions were still hard and wages were not high, the most glaring deficiency in Dundee, in the second quarter of the century, was the lack of adequate housing for the rapidly growing population. The 1793 statistical account claimed, with some pride, that the council "has exerted itself to promote the public good. The building and endowing of new churches, the paving and lighting of streets, the opening of new ones, especially a new passage to the shore, the building of new piers, and the general improvement of the harbour, are works which they have executed within these 10 or 12 years, and which are both of great importance and entitle them to no small share of praise."[23] While the appearance of the town may have seemed more impressive to the visitor, however, this did nothing to improve living conditions for the workers. The same 1793 account went on to state: "The principal causes of unhealthiness in Dundee, are the height of the houses, the narrowness of the tenements and of some streets, by which the people are too much crowded upon one another."[24] The account went on to describe the greater part of the families as "living by half-dozens...under the same roof, with common stairs, without back yards or courts, and many possessing only single rooms." There were next to no parks or open spaces to which people could resort to get a breath of fresh air.[25]

Forty years later the housing situation was much more acute. There is no accurate figure for the number of houses being built until after the 1851 census, though it has been claimed that "in spite of a rise in population of 30,000 between 1841 and 1861, only 568 new houses were built."[26] Dundee was building upward. Typical of the time were the four stories and attics, accommodating fifteen or sixteen families in one- or two-room houses at a rent of two, three,

---

23. *Dundee in 1793 and 1833*, 37.
24. *Dundee in 1793 and 1833*, 8–9.
25. *Dundee in 1793 and 1833*, 52.
26. Whately, Swinfen, and Smith, *Life and Times of Dundee*, 106.

or four pounds per week.[27] Long after "successive commissions deplored their existence," Dundee (along with Glasgow) continued to build "single-ends," one-room apartments. These were deemed to be adequate for some families and could also be justified in the light of the large number of spinster mill girls. There were also cellar dwellings known as "sunk flats" below pavement level.[28]

## Segregation of the Classes

Another unfortunate feature, certainly from the point of view of church life and fellowship, was the way in which, as workers crowded into the town, the upper class tended to move away from the working areas. This led to a segregation of the classes. In December 1840, Reverend George Lewis of St. David's Church gave a series of lectures in the Watt Institute on the physical, educational, and moral statistics of Dundee. He commented on the effect of class movement as follows: "There is moral and social distance between the dwellers at the extremities of our cities, greater far than the physical distance between the centre and extremities of the island; it were easier to construct a moral bridge between Dundee and the remotest of our Western Isles, than between its own extremes."[29] In his parish membership there was a small middle class and an even smaller upper class, which had taken to commuting in to town, using the recently developed railway lines.[30] The result was that there was no interaction between rich and poor. In the opinion of Lewis, "One of the

---

27. Enid Gauldie, *Cruel Habitations: A History of Working-Class Housing 1780– 1918* (London: Allen and Unwin, 1974), 172.

28. Gauldie, *Cruel Habitations*, 95, 162.

29. George Lewis, *The State of St. David's Parish, with remarks on the Moral and Physical Statistics of Dundee* (Dundee, Scotland: William Middleton, 1841), 3.

30. Dundee-Newtyle was the earliest, begun in 1833. The Dundee-Arbroath line was opened in October 1838. S. G. E. Lythe, "The Dundee and Newtyle Railway," *The Railway Magazine* (August 1951): 548–50; Peter F. Marshall, *The Railways of Dundee* (Oxford: Oakwood Press, 1996), 17–20; S. G. E. Lythe, "Early Days of the Arbroath and Forfar Railways," *The Railway Magazine* (January/February 1953): 55–57; and *Dundee, Perth, and Cupar Advertiser*, October 12, 1838; April 3, 1840.

great evils in St. David's Parish, in common with other manufacturing districts, is the want of a mixture of different ranks of society."[31]

The town houses of the local upper-class members were vacated for the more pleasant, nearby country areas. Their houses were often turned into tenements or inns. For example, Sir John Ogilvy moved out of the city center to the Baldovan area on the north bank of the Dighty Burn.[32]

## The Health of the Working Classes Was Affected

The health of the working classes was greatly affected by their living conditions. The 1793 statistical account regarded Dundee as "a very healthy place," where "fevers are seldom infectious, and agues almost unknown."[33] Forty years later, however, the 1833 account would observe that malignant cholera afflicted the town in "two eruptions, one in July [1832], the other in October...carrying off 512 persons out of 808 seized."[34]

Increasingly in the 1830s and 1840s, concern was expressed over mortality from various diseases, particularly among the working class. Although the classes were largely segregated, well-meaning citizens sought to raise awareness in the press. In September 1837, one correspondent to the *Advertiser*, commenting on the medical report of the infirmary for the previous year, wrote of 1,009 cases, with 251 in surgery, making a total of 1,260. The article went on to state, "The mortality in Dundee last year...is far greater than in any other large manufacturing towns, such as Manchester, Liverpool, Glasgow, and nearly twice as great as the average of Scotland." Of the 1,009 cases, no fewer than seven hundred were cases of typhus fever. Fifty had died of smallpox.[35] Just after the arrival of McCheyne

---

31. George Lewis, *The Tavern Bill of Dundee, and what might be made of it* (Dundee, Scotland: William Middleton, 1841), 9.

32. Lenman, Lythe, and Gauldie, *Dundee and Its Textile Industry*, 4, 10.

33. *Dundee in 1793 and 1833*, 9 (1793 account).

34. *Dundee in 1793 and 1833*, 67.

35. *Dundee, Perth, and Cupar Advertiser*, September 8, 1837.

in Dundee, the *Advertiser* carried an article on the state of health in Dundee:

> Since the commencement of the Bill of Mortality in November last, the state of disease and the number of deaths have been very heavy. The average of deaths for a year or two back has been about thirty-two weekly; but from the rapid increase of our population this year, particularly in those classes which from various causes, are most liable to be attacked with fever, etc., a rather higher average may have been expected. For some weeks back the deaths have been about fifty; and in the week ending on Saturday last it rose as high as ninety-six. The mortality since then has rather increased than diminished. The diseases most prevalent and fatal during the above period have been the measles, consumption, smallpox, and various kinds of fever.... In general, the greatest mortality has taken place among the old and infirm, and amongst children.[36]

Reverend Lewis calculated that from 1833 to 1839 there were 11,808 cases of fever in Dundee, resulting in 1,312 deaths. This meant that fever took away more than a tenth of the population. The average mortality in Dundee in those years, 1833 to 1839, was one in thirty-two annually, whereas the Scottish average was one in forty-five.[37]

Repeatedly, comparison was made between the state of health in Dundee and in other cities. One concerned correspondent, in an article titled "One of Seventy Thousand," wrote to the *Advertiser* of "the alarming state of public health of the town—the prevalence of the malignant disease called typhus fever." He went on to comment, "No other conclusion can be come to than that there is something radically wrong in the sanitary regulations of this crowded town. Diseases rage in other cities, but it is only in Dundee where they assume a peculiar virulent character and where they find a permanent abode."[38] The authorities were slow to act in the matter. In 1820, surgeon William Dick, in his *Remarks on Endemic Fever*, had recommended the setting

---

36. *Dundee, Perth, and Cupar Advertiser*, January 6, 1837.
37. Lewis, *State of St. David's Parish*, 41, 44–45.
38. *Dundee, Perth, and Cupar Advertiser*, January 8, 1840.

up of a local board of health.[39] Once set up, the board ordered, in 1832, during the outbreak of cholera, a general fumigation of the town. Tar barrels were to be placed at different points in the street, and set fire to.[40] A decade later, in 1842, Dundee received, along with every town and burgh in the land, a copy of the sanitary report of the poor law commissioners. Nothing was done to implement the various reforms suggested. An *Advertiser* editorial for January 1843 claimed that neither the authorities nor "benevolence" had acted. "The Report...is, so far as regards this town and neighbourhood, a dead letter." Not only was the report ignored, but no effort was made to "ascertain the possibility of curing these evils. Fever continues to hold high festival and the Authorities continue to cry for more money."[41]

Robert Murray McCheyne, fully aware of the brevity of life and the more unhealthy and stressful locality in which he was now placed, took advantage in his ministry of the death from fever of several in his parish. Preaching a sermon on the brevity of life titled "Death's Lessons," from Job 14:1–2, he said:

> We have had solemn experience of these truths in these few days. There have been five solemn deaths, all connected with our parish, and taken together, they form a practical commentary on these words. Two children died, both lovely and pleasant in their lives.... A young man in his prime...has been sent away. Another was the blooming mother of eight blooming children, beloved and admired by all around her, with all this world could give to make her happy: but the cry came at midnight.... The last was an aged man, called upon, after long forbearance, to give his account. How solemn the lesson! The child, the young man, the mother, the hoary head—all laid low this day! Man that is born of a woman is of few days.[42]

39. William Dick, *Remarks on Epidemic fever, commonly called Typhus* (Dundee, Scotland: Alexander Colville, 1820), 12, 63–71.

40. *Dundee, Perth, and Cupar Advertiser*, October 4, 1832.

41. *Dundee, Perth, and Cupar Advertiser*, January 27, 1843.

42. R. M. McCheyne, *From the Preacher's Heart: Sermons and Lectures of Robert Murray McCheyne* (Fearn, Scotland: Christian Focus, 2001), 348–49. Preached February 20, 1843.

Shortly after this, McCheyne himself caught typhus fever while engaged in his regular pastoral duties and was called home on March 25, 1843. The years 1842 to 1843 were a particularly bad time for typhus fever. The King Street Infirmary, first opened in 1798, could not cope with increased admissions. By the 1840s it was declared "utterly inadequate." It was not until 1855 that the new Dundee Royal Infirmary was opened.[43]

In the meantime, with people constantly crowding into the town, the situation in St. David's Parish was drawn to the attention of Dr. Arrott, physician at the Infirmary, by one of Reverend Lewis's elders. He described how three families, comprising fifteen people in total, were crammed into two small, badly ventilated rooms. Another three families, making up sixteen people altogether, were housed in two similar small rooms. Dr. Arrott took two of Lewis's elders with him to verify for himself. He found 129 persons crowded into 27 rooms, "being rather more than four persons to each room. 101 of the 129 had fever." He pointed out the contrast by observing that while in the Scouringburn area seven dwelt in a room 15 feet by 11 feet, with only one bed and one set of bed clothes, just down from the Infirmary in King Street, 42 inhabitants lived in 93 rooms, that is, two rooms to each person, and no fever cases.[44]

## The Water Question

Another problem that affected Dundee more than some other towns found expression in what became known as the "water question." There was a desperate need for water to be supplied from outside the town. Peter Carmichael recorded how Dundee was in a "state of turmoil over the water question": "All were agreed that the nine ancient wells within the burgh supplemented as they were by carts from the country which sold water at the rate of four pitcherfuls for a penny, had become altogether inadequate for the supply of the town."[45] At first there was agreement that the Dighty Burn and its tributaries to

---

43. Whately, Swinfen, and Smith, *Life and Times of Dundee*, 107.

44. *Dundee, Perth, and Cupar Advertiser*, April 14, 1843.

45. Peter Carmichael Biographical Works, 234–35.

the north of Dundee should be used to provide an adequate supply of water. Business interests, however, killed this idea: mill owners and the water caddies opposed it as they saw their livelihood threatened.

In 1836, civil engineer and water consultant George Buchanan of Edinburgh was brought in to advise. He proposed drawing a supply of water from the River Isla twelve miles away to a reservoir at Dundee Law. He had the backing of a London consultant also.[46] Others, however, favored using the water at Monikie as a source of supply. The matter dragged on because the authorities could not agree as to whether a privately owned joint stock company should have the responsibility for providing the water, or if it should be financed by a publicly owned water commission that would assess all householders.[47] The "Water War," as it had become known, raged, and in the process the town went further into debt, leading to the bankruptcy of the corporation between 1842 and 1864.[48] It was not until 1845 that progress was made with the Dundee Water Act, which initially provided a "highly unsatisfactory supply of water, from Monikie and Stobsmuir."[49] Only as late as 1876 could the chamber of commerce claim that Dundee now had a piped supply sufficient for all domestic and industrial purposes.[50]

## Years of Trade Depression and Unemployment
What added to the difficulties of the inhabitants of Dundee in the 1830s and 1840s was the instability of the market for cloth. This led to great unemployment. During the decade from 1826 to 1836 there

46. George Buchanan, *Abstract of Report on the Proposed Plan for supplying the Town of Dundee with water* (Dundee, Scotland: D. Hill and Son, 1836), 3–4; W. Cubitt, *Report on the Plan for supplying the Town of Dundee with water, as proposed by G. Buchanan, esq. Edinburgh, Civil Engineer* (Dundee, Scotland: D. Hill and Son, 1836), 4–5.

47. *Charters, Writs, and Public Documents of the Royal Burgh of Dundee, the Hospital and Johnston's Bequest: 1292–1880* (Dundee, Scotland: D. R. Clark and Son, 1880), 225–26; Whately, Swinfen, and Smith, *Life and Times of Dundee,* 138.

48. Carmichael, *Dundee Textile Industry,* 15.

49. Whately, Swinfen, and Smith, *Life and Times of Dundee,* 107.

50. Lenman, Lythe, and Gauldie, *Dundee and Its Textile Industry,* 9.

was a rapid growth of manufactures, with abundant employment and good wages for workers. The years 1833 to 1836, in particular, were a period of great commercial prosperity. Then, in September 1836, a great stagnation of trade began, resulting in the closure of mills and unemployment for operatives. The pattern was set for several years. In November 1839 the *Advertiser* noted that the unemployed amounted to nearly two thousand and was increasing daily.[51] Upward of twenty mills were closed, and others were not working at anything like full capacity. The following year the *Advertiser* remarked, in the local intelligence columns:

> We have seldom known our trade more depressed than at the present time…. The demand for flax is very languid indeed at our notations; yarns are also in slack demand, and are if anything a shade lower in price. The accounts from America, our most extensive market for linens, are far from encouraging, and the low rates for cotton goods form a strong opposition to a demand for flax and linens.[52]

Peter Carmichael recorded the year 1841 ending in gloom, and that "the trade of the country continued in a state of depression throughout 1842."[53] Other trades were also affected. By 1842 the number of mechanics (workers in metal) working was a quarter of what it had been in 1837.[54] Half those in shipbuilding were out of work. Of 159 journeymen tailors, only five were in full employment.[55] The only people who seemed to benefit were the innkeepers. Reverend Lewis commented, "Of all the trades of Dundee, the publican seems to have the lion's share of the poor man's earnings."[56] The number of unemployed soon exceeded four thousand.

---

51. *Dundee, Perth, and Cupar Advertiser*, November 29, 1839.

52. *Dundee, Perth, and Cupar Advertiser*, April 10, 1840.

53. Peter Carmichael Biographical Works, 260–61.

54. Carmichael, *Dundee Textile Industry*, 86.

55. *Report of the Great Anti-Corn Law meeting held at Dundee, on Thursday, 6th Jan. 1842* (Dundee, Scotland: J. Chalmers, Wm. Livingstone and F. Shaw, 1842), v, vi.

56. George Lewis, *The Pauper Bill of Dundee, and what should be done with it* (Dundee, Scotland: William Middleton, 1841), 5.

As work became scarce, for some emigration was an attractive alternative to struggling to survive at home. At the end of 1836, the *Advertiser* carried a notice offering free passage to New South Wales, with a guarantee of one year's employment, for married mechanics age thirty-five and under, with families and unmarried female connections between eighteen and thirty. The following year 328 Dundonians took advantage of free passage on the specially chartered *John Barry*. This was the start of a continuous stream of emigration.[57]

## Attempts to Relieve the Distressed Poor

How to relieve the distressed poor was a major headache for the authorities in those years. In 1832 the number of paupers requiring assistance stood at 744. By June 1842 it had risen to 1,761. What augmented the problem was that "almost all the poor of the county take refuge in the towns."[58] As the number of poor and unemployed requiring assistance increased, a meeting of the magistrates, heritors, and general kirk session set up a committee to report on pauperism in Dundee. The convener was P. H. Thoms, an elder of St. Peter's Church. Up to 1845 it was the responsibility of kirk sessions to provide poor relief. In that year a Poor Law Amendment Act gave local authorities the right to impose assessments on property holders.[59] Meanwhile, the committee recommended "laying the assessment upon means and substance, or upon real rents and incomes combined." Most of the churches had "monthly pensioners" to support. Chapelshade Parish had the highest number at 149, and St. David's was a close second with 131. Expenses were also incurred by the parish in looking after children abandoned by their parents. In St. David's there were 336

---

57. *Dundee, Perth, and Cupar Advertiser*, December 2, 1836; March 24, 1837; and August 17, 1968. The 1968 article, "To Australia the Hard Way in 1837," referred to forty deaths on board the *John Barry*, including twenty-seven children. There was an eight-week wait before landing, because typhus was diagnosed on board. Carmichael, *Dundee Textile Industry*, 83n1.

58. *Dundee, Perth, and Cupar Advertiser*, June 17, 1842; July 1, 1842.

59. J. H. S. Burleigh, *A Church History of Scotland* (Oxford: Oxford University Press, 1960), 381–82.

widows, which meant every sixth family was deprived of its father. The kirk session also took responsibility for boarders in the asylum.[60] During the stressful years of the late 1830s and early 1840s, the churches found it increasingly difficult to provide for the poor from their weekly collections.

Various public meetings were held, in the Magdalen Yard Green[61] and in the town hall, to consider additional means of relieving destitution. One suggestion was relief in the form of outdoor work developing Magdalen Yard Green, which was undertaken. Another suggestion, which showed the paternalistic attitude to poverty in early Victorian times, was to set up a committee and open a subscription for the purpose of supplying food and coals to those most in need. Eight soup kitchens were set up. Other enterprises included a ball in the Thistle Hall and an oratorio and other amateur performances for the benefit of unemployed operatives. The annual soiree of the Mariners' Abstinence Society was devoted to helping the unemployed.[62]

## Political Agitation

It is not surprising that, given the distress of those years, many in Dundee were attracted to political movements of the time. The Chartist Movement, arising out of disappointment with the Great Reform Act of 1832,[63] was strong in Dundee, drawing much of its support and leadership from textiles workers. Public meetings were held to

---

60. *Report on the Pauperism of Dundee: by a committee appointed at a meeting of the magistrates, heritors, and general session* (Dundee, Scotland: David Hill, at the Courier Office, 1839), 3, 4, 23; General Kirk-Session Minutes, March 29, 1837; March 14, 1838; April 7, 1842; March 6, 8, 1843, Dundee City Archives, MS CH3/338/ 5; Lewis, *Tavern Bill of Dundee*, 9; and *List of the Poor of Dundee from 1st January to 31st December 1840*, comp. Tay Valley Family History Society, 2007, CD-ROM.

61. Whately, Swinfen, and Smith, *Life and Times of Dundee*, 141.

62. *Dundee, Perth, and Cupar Advertiser*, June 16, 23, 1837; March 2, 1838; November 22, 1839; January 8, 10, 1840; April 3, 1840; March 25, 1842; June 17, 1842; July 1, 1842.

63. The Chartist Movement, which lasted from 1838 to 1858, took its name from the People's Charter of 1838, which called for (1) votes for all men over twenty-one years of age, of sound mind and not undergoing punishment for a crime; (2) voting by secret ballot; (3) abolition of property qualifications for members of Parliament

agitate for universal male suffrage and the secret ballot.[64] Chartist activity moved from meetings to demonstrations. In June 1839, seven to eight hundred trades lads, with flags and bands of music, processed from the Nethergate to Magdalen Yard Green with their Chartist demands.[65] The following year a Chartist church was set up, meeting on Lindsay Street, with John Duncan as their preacher.[66] If a petition of 20,523 signatures to commute the death sentence of a Welsh Chartist is to be taken at face value, their strength in Dundee made them a force to be reckoned with; this was more than a third of the entire population.[67] David Robertson suggested that "to some extent they regarded themselves as being in competition with evangelicals like McCheyne for the affections of the working class."[68]

In spite of the presence of radical "physical force" promoted by Chartist leader Feargus O'Connor in Dundee in October 1841, the local Chartists stuck to "moral persuasion," only small elements being desirous of using force. Nor did they heed the Chartist National Convention's call for a month of "idle begging" (a sacred month), or even two or three days' withdrawal of labor.[69] There was one notable incident that hit the newspapers. Some Chartist leaders were indicted for the crimes of mobbing, rioting, and breach of the peace, "to the great terror and alarm of the lieges." For disrupting a church defense meeting, the leaders got four months in jail.[70]

Concurrent with Chartist agitation was the work of the Anti-Corn Law League. One of the leaders was Edward Baxter of Baxter Brothers Mill. In Dundee the league was comprised of local merchants, manu-

---

(MPs); (4) payment of MPs; (5) equal electoral districts; and (6) annual parliamentary elections.

64. *Dundee, Perth, and Cupar Advertiser*, April and December 1837.

65. *Dundee, Perth, and Cupar Advertiser*, June 21, 1839.

66. *Dundee, Perth, and Cupar Advertiser*, September 25, 1840.

67. Robertson, *Awakening*, 87.

68. Robertson, *Awakening*, 88.

69. Peter Carmichael Biographical Works, 257–58; Carmichael, *Dundee Textile Industry*, 81–82.

70. *Dundee, Perth, and Cupar Advertiser*, January 6, 1843; *Dundee Warder and Arbroath and Forfar Journal*, January 24, 1843.

facturers, and shipowners. They had one aim—to get the Corn Laws repealed, laws that had kept grain prices artificially high to benefit landowners and making it difficult for workers to afford bread. Since the workers could not afford meat, many subsisted on a diet of meal and potatoes.[71] At the Great Anti-Corn Law Meeting in Dundee on January 6, 1842, it was declared that "taxes on food and prohibitory duties on foreign productions, were the great cause of the present distress. Freedom of trade was the inalienable right of free men."[72] For a time Chartists and Leaguers had a precarious alliance, but before long the Chartists "denounced the Anti-Corn Law movement as a middle class ramp."[73]

## Neglect of the Poor by the Rich

Another feature of those troubled years was a growing estrangement between the working-class poor and the upper classes, the latter neglecting the former. The *Dundee Warder* commented on this in February 1841:

> The poor have indeed been long and cruelly neglected by the rich, who too generally have acted as if the possession of riches brought not with it the solemn duty of extending the liberal hand of aid and sympathy to the many ever around them suffering from the pangs of want and nakedness. The dwellings of the destitute have been left unvisited, and the poor having ceased to know the rich as benefactors, have come to regard them as enemies and oppressors; and hence has arisen that feeling of enmity and bitterness that so unhappily exists between different classes of the community, and which threatens to prove so disastrous in its consequences to the welfare and stability of society.[74]

Later that same year, in a column on the state of the poor fund in Dundee, the *Warder* referred to the "fearfully growing demoralization

---

71. Lenman, Lythe, and Gauldie, *Dundee and Its Textile Industry*, 18.
72. *Report of the Great Anti-Corn Law meeting*, 2.
73. Lenman, Lythe, and Gauldie, *Dundee and Its Textile Industry*, 18.
74. *Dundee Warder*, February 9, 1841.

of the poor," as witnessed by the increased numbers of illegitimate children, families deserted by one or both parents, and the excessive intemperance that characterized the poor. All of this led to a drain on the resources of the poor fund, "without making a felt or perceptible diminution, or even alleviation, of the destitution and misery it is meant to cure." The newspaper was clear as to the remedy: "The evil, to almost nine-tenths of its extent, arises from moral causes, and the agencies to remove them must be moral likewise. We must make the character of the poor better, if we wish to make pauperism less."[75] This paternalistic statement was typical of the thinking of many in early Victorian times. It took no account of the living conditions of many in Dundee or of the deprivation caused by unemployment or low wages.

## McCheyne Speaks Out

Such, then, was the distressing state of Dundee to which Robert Murray McCheyne, with his privileged middle-class upbringing in the New Town of Edinburgh, came in November 1836. He himself believed very much in the social order of the day, with its different classes. Toward the end of his life he wrote: "The lower orders are very well in their way, but should be kept in their place. You will say, 'What pride! We are all alike in the eyes of God.' So we are; but, as long as we are in this world, it is our duty to keep up the distinctions of rank."[76] With regard to the conditions that he found in Dundee, he linked this in his thinking with the town's departure in large measure from the living God. In a Fast Day sermon on Isaiah 22:12–14, delivered on May 7, 1840, he declared:

> This town in special manner has been visited by commercial distress—poverty, one of the sorest curses that God sends, lies heavy on us…. This very poverty is a call to set apart a season for humbling—and God may lift away the stroke…. I have no

---

75. *Dundee Warder*, November 30, 1841.

76. Alexander Smellie, *Robert Murray McCheyne* (Fearn, Scotland: Christian Focus, 1995), 141.

confidence in poor laws or any change in our laws benefitting
the poor—as long as we are under God's displeasure.[77]

Nor did he rise, in his thinking, to embrace a scheme like that which
Dr. Chalmers attempted to introduce, with only limited success, in the
West Port area of Edinburgh, a scheme to alleviate inner-city poverty.[78]

Nevertheless, McCheyne had a heart for the poor of Dundee,
which found expression in at least two ways. One of the features of
his few short years in the city was his constant interaction with the
working-class people who largely made up his parish. This is seen
especially in his methodical and conscientious visitation work
(expanded on in chapter 3). He also expressed his feelings and concern for the poor in his sermons. After little more than a year in
Dundee, he preached a sermon titled "The Blessedness of Giving,"
from the words of Christ in Acts 20:35, "It is more blessed to give
than to receive." He let the few wealthier members of his congregation know just what he thought of them for their neglect of the poor:

> Oh, my dear Christians! If you would be like Christ, give
> much, give often, give freely, to the vile and the poor, the
> thankless and the undeserving. Christ is glorious and happy,
> and so will you be. It is not your money I want, but your hap-
> piness. Remember his own words: "It is more blessed to give
> than to receive."... Your haughty dwelling rises in the midst of
> thousands who have scarce a fire to warm themselves at, and
> have but little clothing to keep out the biting frost; and yet
> you never darken their door. You heave a sigh, perhaps at a
> distance; but you do not visit them. Ah, my dear friends! I am
> concerned for the poor; but more for you. I know not what
> Christ will say to you in the great day. You seem to be Chris-
> tians, and yet you care not for his poor. Oh, what a change will
> pass upon you as you enter the gates of heaven! You will be

77. R. M. McCheyne, *The Passionate Preacher: Sermons of Robert Murray McCheyne* (Fearn, Scotland: Christian Focus, 1999), 45–49.

78. S. J. Brown, "The Disruption and Urban Poverty: Thomas Chalmers and the West Port Operation in Edinburgh, 1844–47," *Records of the Scottish Church History Society* 20 (1978): 65–89.

saved, but that will be all. There will be no abundant entrance for you: "He that soweth sparingly shall reap also sparingly."[79]

In another sermon on the Great Commission ("Go ye into all the world"), his missionary heart, with its passion for souls, showed itself clearly, as he sought to stir up his congregation to be active in reaching out to the multitude of unevangelized around St. Peter's: "This is what we need in this town—a ministry that will go to seek the people. We need men with the compassion of Christ who will leave home, friends, comforts all behind and go into the haunts of profligacy, the dens of the Cowgate, and with the love and life of Jesus persuade them to turn and not die."[80] Dundee in the 1830s and 1840s was a place of prosperity for part of the time for those in business such as factory owners. It was, however, a place of much social and economic distress for the vast number of the fast-growing population of the town. In the providence and grace of God, however, many of the young and many of the poor, who would not live long into adult life, were in particular blessed to be awakened and converted in those revival years.

---

79. McCheyne, *From the Preacher's Heart,* 395–96.
80. McCheyne, *Passionate Preacher,* 136–41.

# Two Background Religious Issues of the Times

In our town, I suppose there are at the least 15,000 still living in practical heathenism without having a pastor to look after them. I bless God that there are two new churches nearly ready to be opened and trust all God's children will pray that we may get pastors after God's own heart. Still, what are these among so many? I do wonder that Christians who have money can live at ease and see these multitudes going down. It is a crying sin.

—Robert Murray McCheyne, a Fast Day
sermon on Isaiah 22:12–14

In regard to the great public questions that were then shaking the Church of Scotland, his views were decided and unhesitating. No policy, in his view, could be more ruinous to true Christianity, or more fitted to blight vital godliness, than that of Moderatism. He once wrote to a friend in Ireland: "You don't know what Moderatism is. It's a plant that our heavenly Father never planted, and I trust it is now to be rooted up." The great question of the Church's independence of the civil power in all matters spiritual, and the right of the Christian people to judge if the pastor appointed over them had the Shepherd's voice, he invariably held to be part of Scripture truth; which, therefore, must be preached and carried into practice at all hazards. In like manner he rejoiced exceedingly in the settlements of faithful minsters.

—Andrew A. Bonar, *Memoir and Remains
of the Rev. Robert Murray McCheyne*

At the beginning of the nineteenth century, one of the desperate needs of the Scottish church, particularly in those areas of vastly increased population, was the creation of new parishes to cater to masses of unchurched people. The first step to remedy this situation consisted of appointing extra ministers to existing churches so that they became collegiate.[1] The next step was the building and endowing, by private enterprise, of what were known as "chapels-of-ease." These chapels had no area assigned to them and no kirk session of their own. They did, however, provide much-needed accommodation in those days.[2]

In 1828 Dr. Thomas Chalmers was appointed convenor of a committee on church accommodation. Once the evangelical party gained ascendancy in the General Assembly after 1834, the committee was able to make good headway and raised two hundred thousand pounds for the creation of two hundred new parishes. According to the 1833 statistical account, Dundee had at least twenty-six different places of worship.[3] It was estimated, however, that in Dundee as many as nine thousand people had no church connection of any kind.[4] The prime mover in the matter of church extension in Dundee was Reverend John Roxburgh, who came to St. John's, or the Cross Kirk, the fourth Established charge, in 1834. He grasped the situation quickly. He had come to a parish with a population of six thousand in addition to his own congregation. There was desperate need for church extension in the west end of his parish. Early in 1835, a circular was sent

---

1. Burleigh, *Church History*, 319.

2. A. L. Drummond and James Bulloch, *The Scottish Church 1688–1843* (Edinburgh: St. Andrews Press, 1981), 185–86.

3. The account is actually for the year 1832, though published in 1833. It records the existence of the following: eight Established Church congregations and three chapels-of-ease; four Seceding congregations; one Congregational chapel; one of Scotch Independents; one Relief chapel; one Methodist chapel; one Scotch Baptist; two other small Baptist groups; one Glassite church, the largest congregation in the town, formed by John Glas after he was deposed from Tealing Church of Scotland; two Episcopal chapels and one Roman Catholic church of mainly Irish people. *Dundee in 1793 and 1833*, 42–43.

4. *History of St. Peter's Free Church, Dundee* (Dundee, Scotland: Alexander Ewan, 1886), 3.

from St. John's to the other Established congregations, asking them to "unite heartily" in a scheme for church extension, for the population of Dundee had increased by about twenty thousand souls from 1821 to 1835.[5] Many of the existing parishes were too large, a problem Dundee ministers did not hesitate to point out. Once settled in St. Peter's, McCheyne delivered a sermon titled "Reasons for Lack of Success in Our Day." In it he said, "The flocks are too large to be cared for by the Shepherd. My own flock is just four times the size a flock used to be in the days of our fathers, so that I am called upon to do the work of four ministers, and left like Issachar, crouching beneath two burdens."[6] Reverend George Lewis, inducted to St. David's Church in February 1839, was "entirely opposed to the principle of allotting more than two thousand souls to the care of more than one minister."[7] He took advantage of the occasion of the burning down, on January 3, 1841, of three of the four city churches clustered together downtown, to suggest there should be four parish churches of one thousand sittings each, "free from the incubus of seat-rents, and divisible amongst a parish not exceeding 2,000 souls."[8]

A second problem, referred to above, was seat rents. The circular from St. John's answered the objection to the erection of new church buildings by pointing out that seat rents in city churches are "so high, as practically to exclude the families of the working classes."[9] The circular was making a valid point here with regard to gospel outreach in the neighborhood. Just two years earlier, a correspondent to the *Dundee Chronicle* complained of seat letting, "even by auction!":

---

5. Managers Minutes of St. Peter's Church, 1835–1843, Dundee City Archives, MS CH3/338/5.

6. McCheyne, *From the Preacher's Heart*, 89 (February 25, 1838).

7. Kirk-Session Records of St. David's Parish Church, Dundee, 1834–1877, Dundee City Archives, MS CH2/926/1; *Dundee Warder*, December 7, 1841, reporting on an ordinary meeting of the Presbytery of Dundee.

8. George Lewis, *The Church in the Fire, and out of the Fire* (Dundee, Scotland: William Middleton, 1841), 2, 16.

9. Managers' Minutes of St. Peter's Church.

Now, sir, is this as it should be? Is this, "Ho, every one that thirsteth?" See that poor frail woman hanging over the door of that empty pew, which she is not permitted to enter; or resting with the Bible in her lap, on the cold step of a stone stair, where she can neither see nor hear to the purpose; and has she no right to better accommodation in a house built and supported expressly for her? The churches of the Dissenters have been filled by the operation of this evil.[10]

McCheyne came to recognize that seat rents were keeping people away and advocated their complete removal, or at least their reduction to what the poor could afford.[11] His colleague George Lewis commented that "in times of trade depression, the seat rent is often the first thing to be given up."[12]

For the above reasons, the Dundee presbyterial committee on church extension went ahead with its work, in spite of strong protest and objection from congregations of Dissenters at having to pay for the funding of Established Church buildings.[13] McCheyne was both enthusiastic and optimistic: "We are building in this town new churches, and we want ministers, and we are apt to fear that we may not succeed; but let us trust Christ, let us go forward in power, let us go forward in simple faith, looking unto Jesus."[14] In November 1838 John Baxter was ordained to the new working-class parish of Hilltown. The parish of Wallacetown was constituted in October 1839 and the following May was opened for public worship. In September 1840, Patrick Miller, formerly a missionary in St. David's Parish, was

---

10. *Dundee Chronicle*, December 11, 1832. Article signed by Presbyter, St. Andrews.

11. Robert Murray McCheyne to his father, August 14, 1838, MACCH 2.1.

12. Lewis, *State of St. David's Parish*, 12.

13. James R. McGavin, speech delivered at the Anti-Church Endowment Meeting, held in Ward Chapel, Dundee, February 27, 1838, 6; *Report of the Speeches delivered at the Anti-Endowment Meeting, held in George's Chapel, Dundee, December 27, 1838* (Dundee, Scotland: Advertiser Office, 1839), 11.

14. R. M. McCheyne, *Brief Expositions of the Epistles to the Seven Churches of Asia* (Glasgow: N. Adsheed and Son, 1958), 42–43.

ordained there.[15] Then in April 1841 Alexander McPherson took up his duties as minister of the new Dudhope Parish Church.[16]

There was now a nucleus of evangelical Church of Scotland ministers in the town who would work most harmoniously together during the awakening and beyond. It was said of Roxburgh, the first of the group to be settled, that he "greatly valued the aid derived from the earnest spiritual pleadings, both in the Presbytery and in public, of his friend and brother, Mr McCheyne, whose devout mind deeply felt how much the interests of vital godliness were concerned in the preservation of the principles for which the Church was contending."[17] Even, however, with the Established Church extension program in operation and the Free Church building program begun after 1843, Dundee, with a population of 81,494 in 1851, had seating for only 44.8 percent of its people. It has, therefore, been rightly stated that "despite the great expansion of accommodation after 1843, when the Free Church building programme got under way, the churches generally were still far short of tackling the problem of population explosion within the traditional parochial boundaries."[18]

## Lay Patronage and the Spiritual Independence of the Church

There had always been an evangelical succession of outstanding ministers throughout the eighteenth and early nineteenth centuries: men such as Thomas Halyburton, minister of Ceres in Fife from 1700 to 1710, then professor of divinity at St. Andrews;[19] and Dr. John

---

15. Dundee Presbytery Minutes, November 8, 1838; July 3, 1839; October 2, 1839, Dundee City Archives, MS CH2/103; Hew Scott, ed., *Fasti Ecclesiae Scoticanae*, vol. 5, *Synod of Fife and Angus and the Mearns* (Edinburgh: Oliver and Boyd, 1925), 341; and *Dundee, Perth, and Cupar Advertiser*, September 25, 1840.

16. Scott, *Fasti Ecclesiae Scoticanae*, 5:313; Dundee Presbytery Minutes, February 2, 1842; and Andrew Inglis, *Notes of the History of Dudhope Free Church, Lochee Road, Dundee* (Dundee, Scotland: James P. Matthew, 1890), 8.

17. Thomas Brown, *Annals of the Disruption* (Edinburgh: MacNiven and Wallace, 1893), 16.

18. A. Allan Maclaren, *Religion and Social Class* (London: Routledge and Kegan Paul, 1974), 37.

19. Scott, *Fasti Ecclesiae Scoticanae*, 5:132.

Erskine, minister of Old Greyfriars Church, Edinburgh. Though born into a wealthy family, Erskine chose the pastorate, for he saw it as "a sacred office for the purpose of guiding individuals to eternal salvation."[20] For him the whole center of preaching was the "doctrine of Christ crucified." In Dundee there was John Willison, to whom McCheyne was compared. Minister of South Church from 1716 to 1750, he was one of the most prominent and respected ministers of his day. His pastoral writings for young and old were for a long time favorite reading with the Christian public.[21] The visits of Whitefield and the Wesleys and the work of other godly ministers saw awakenings in various parts of Scotland, such as at Kilsyth and Cambuslang. Recent research has shown just how extensive this was, not only in Lowland Scotland, but also in the Highlands.[22] The impact of brothers James and Robert Haldane and their home missionaries in the late eighteenth and early nineteenth centuries "added a massive impetus to evangelicalism in the country."[23]

In the days of Burns and McCheyne, however, the church in Scotland was still slowly emerging from the age of the Moderates.

---

20. Hew Scott, ed., *Fasti Ecclesiae Scotinae*, vol. 1, *Synod of Lothian and Tweeddale* (Edinburgh: Oliver & Boyd, 1925), 34, 47–48; Jonathan Yeager, "John Erskine (1721–1803): A Scottish Evangelical Minister," *Records of the Scottish Church History Society* 38 (2008): 310.

21. John Willison, *The Mother's Catechism for a Young Child* (Glasgow: John S. Marr and Sons, n.d.); *The Young Communicant's Catechism: or, a Help, both short and plain, for instructing and preparing the Young, to make a right approach to the Lord's Table* (Kilmarnock, Scotland: H. Crawford, 1813); *A Catechism on the Nature and Uses of the Lord's Supper* (Edinburgh: William Whyte, 1842); and *The Afflicted Man's Companion* (London and Edinburgh: Nelson, 1899).

22. John Willison, "Extracts of Attestations, to the Facts in the Narrative, Relating to the Fruits of This Work" (first attestation), in John Gillies, *Historical Collections of Accounts of Revival* (Edinburgh: Banner of Truth Trust, 1981), 436; Lennie, *Land of Many Revivals*, esp. chap. 2. A seminal piece of work was done on the Highlands by John MacInnes, *The Evangelical Movement in the Highlands of Scotland, 1688 to 1800* (Aberdeen: Aberdeen University Press, 1951), esp. chap. 4.

23. Lennie, *Land of Many Revivals*, 171–86; Adam Philip, *The Evangel in Gowrie* (Edinburgh and London: Oliphant, Anderson and Ferrier, 1911), 304. In 1800 St. David's Church, Dundee, was opened by Robert Haldane as a tabernacle. Philip, *Evangel*, 305.

The Patronage Act of 1712 governed the presentation of ministers to parishes. Under the Moderates, many presentees were "intruded" into parish livings, often against the wishes of the parishioners, who opposed their Moderate views. In the eyes of many, patronage became a symbol of the subordination of the church to the upper social orders, especially the landed interest.[24] Those who opposed lay patronage came to be known as Non-Intrusionists. They opposed it primarily because under the Moderate ministers a decline in the evangelical spirit set in, and "there appeared to be a recoil from evangelical doctrine, and a disposition to modify the message of grace."[25] Moderates were critical of preaching that emphasized man's total depravity and utter dependence on God's grace for salvation.[26] They laid stress on themes such as order, rationality, and social progress, emphasizing works as much as faith.[27] They read their sermons as refined compositions, from which the roughness of the old evangelical preaching had been removed.[28] There was a marked decline in those years in the spiritual life of the nation and indifference to spiritual things among many. Pastoral visitation was also neglected greatly.[29] The revival of 1839 took place, therefore, against the backdrop of the climax of a struggle for the spiritual independence of the church.

In the early decades of the nineteenth century, spiritual declension had certainly set in in the Dundee area. One local worthy, writing at the end of the century and looking back over those years, was far from complimentary:

> There was, however, no religious fervour among the people. The ministers as a body, although sincere, lacked enthusiasm.

---

24. S. J. Brown, "The Ten Years' Conflict and the Disruption of 1843," in *Scotland in the Age of Disruption*, ed. S. J. Brown and Michael Fry (Edinburgh: Edinburgh University Press, 1993), 6.

25. W. G. Blaikie, *The Preachers of Scotland, from the Sixth to the Nineteenth Century* (Edinburgh: Banner of Truth Trust, 2001), 202–3.

26. Blaikie, *Preachers of Scotland*, 220.

27. S. J. Brown, *Thomas Chalmers and the Godly Commonwealth* (Oxford: Oxford University Press, 1982), 44.

28. Blaikie, *Preachers of Scotland*, 29, 238.

29. Blaikie, *Preachers of Scotland*, 239–46, 276.

They cultivated the art of literature, and their preaching was of a philosophical and theological nature, the Puritanical earnestness which had hitherto predominated having been substituted by a larger, broader doctrine of Christianity. The term Moderates was applied to them. Besides, in the adminis-tration of the Church, there was no energy. Church extension proceeded slowly, and far behind the face of the growth of the population, and of missionary enterprise abroad the Church had none.[30]

This, then, was the religious climate that Burns and McCheyne inher-ited in the 1830s.

## McCheyne's Views on Moderatism

As can be seen from the quote at the beginning of this chapter, McCheyne had strong views on Moderatism. In his preaching he was particularly critical of those whom he regarded as false shepherds. His addresses on the Good Shepherd (John 10) gave him ample scope to express his beliefs. In his first address, on verses 1–6, he declared, "There is no way in which Satan has done more damage to the Church than by thrusting unfaithful shepherds over the wall of the fold. Such were the Pharisees of old. Such are careless ministers to this day. The false shepherd 'entereth not by the door, but climbeth up some other way.'"[31] He elaborated in verses 6–10 on his belief that it was possible to be possessed of much head knowledge gained at divinity college, yet for there to be no work of grace in the heart:

> Now learning is good, and not to be despised; but it is not the door. Christ is the door of the sheep; and unless a minis-ter enter by this door, he is but a thief and a robber.... Many have entered by the favour of the great, by the patronage of the rich and powerful. They have great influence, and are held in esteem. Still this is not the door: "I am the door of the sheep."[32]

30. James Rollo, *The Ups and Downs of the Church of Scotland in Dundee during the Nineteenth Century* (Dundee, Scotland: [the author], 1902), 1–2.

31. McCheyne, *From the Preacher's Heart*, 512.

32. McCheyne, *From the Preacher's Heart*, 516–17.

McCheyne had no doubt that the hireling of John 10:12–13 repre-
sented unfaithful ministers and urged his congregation to pray that
the true shepherds would be known in a time of heresy or persecution: "Pray...that the day may never dawn on Scotland when it will
be given over to hireling ministers."[33] In his tract "Why Is God a
Stranger in the Land?" the first reason he gave for the silence of God
was unfaithful preaching by ministers to the unconverted, failing to
plead compassionately and warn their hearers to flee from the wrath
to come.[34]

## Non-Intrusion in the Dundee Press, the Town Council, and within the Presbytery

There was strong support for the Non-Intrusionist cause in Dundee.
In 1832, a correspondent to the *Dundee Chronicle* wrote in scathing
terms of the harm he saw patronage doing to church life:

> Patronage crams our kirks with dumb dogs, who neither
> speak eloquently nor impressively from the pulpit. Fair
> enough characters, but who have, as the people express it,
> "mistaken their trade."... Patronage, too, sells kirks. Simony is
> known in various quarters.... Patronage is anti-evangelical in
> its tendencies; it is fond of well-composed moral discourses,
> and cares not a doit about Gospel doctrine. Patronage is the
> parent of sloth and indolence—of daidling, doited, sermon-
> piecing.... It thins kirks and fills change-houses. It is averse
> to parochial visitations and examinations, and either neglects
> them altogether, or slurs them over in a slovenly manner. It
> alienates the hearts of the people, and makes them seek the
> man of their choice.[35]

Two years later, in 1834, the town council declared for the Non-
Intrusionist cause. Two resolutions were passed: first, that it belonged

---

33. R. M. McCheyne, *A Basket of Fragments* (Inverness: Christian Focus, 1979),
20–21.

34. Andrew A. Bonar, *Memoir*, 590–91.

35. *Dundee Chronicle*, Tuesday, December 11, 1832. The *Chronicle* had begun
circulation on October 16, 1832.

to every Christian congregation to choose its own ecclesiastical office-
bearers; second, that the Patronage Act of 1712, which restored the
law of patronage, "has never been received by the people of Scotland
in any other light than an intolerable grievance, and an infringement
on their just rights and liberties."[36]

The Established Church was also strong for the Non-Intrusionist
cause. Petitions were sent to Parliament from the general kirk session of Dundee against intrusion of ministers, requesting legislation
be introduced to avoid further clashes between ecclesiastical and civil
courts.[37] Meetings on behalf of Non-Intrusion were held in several
parishes. After one meeting in St. Peter's, McCheyne remarked that
"he had never had a meeting where there was a deeper and more
solemn feeling." He believed the congregation took the matter of
Non-Intrusion to their prayer meetings and their closets.[38]

There was still, at this time, a small number of Moderates in the
presbytery, led by Dr. David Cannan of Mains of Strathmartine Parish
and Mr. Irvine of Lundie, who were not in favor of petitioning Parliament against intrusion. Nevertheless, by a majority of twenty-three
to seven, the moderator was authorized to proceed. Dr. Cannan's
opposition in particular received an extended entry in the minutes,
and a rebuke to the effect that no minister or elder of the Church of
Scotland should have been providing such opposition in the church's
hour of need.[39]

Matters came to a head nationally when it became clear that the
government was not prepared to accept the claim of right adopted by
the General Assembly in May 1842. This was a five-thousand-word
document in which the church stated its claim to spiritual independence. Dr. Chalmers and several other evangelical leaders organized

---

36. Reported in the *Dundee, Perth, and Cupar Advertiser*, March 28, 1834.

37. General Kirk-Session Minutes, July 4, 1839; January 14, 1840.

38. *Report of the Proceedings at the Meetings of Members and Friends of the
Church of Scotland, in opposition to absolute Patronage and Violent Settlements,
and in defence of the spiritual independence of the church, 28th and 29th January,
1840* (Dundee: William Middleton, 1840); *Dundee Chronicle*, January 30, 1840; and
*Dundee, Perth, and Cupar Advertiser*, January 31, 1840.

39. Dundee Presbytery Minutes, February 5, 1840; April 1, 1840.

a convocation in Edinburgh beginning November 17 and continuing for eight days, at which 465 ministers were present. Two resolutions were passed: one in which they outlined how the church had suffered at the hands of the civil courts, the other declaring they would resign their office and endowments and become part of the Free Church if the Claim of Right was not recognized by Parliament.[40]

McCheyne was present at all the convocation meetings. Bonar recorded that

> he felt the deepest interest in every matter that came before them, got great light as to the path of duty in the course of the consultations, and put his name to all the resolutions, heartily sympathising in the decided determination that, as a Church of Christ, we must abandon our connection with the state, if our "Claim of Rights" (*sic*) were rejected.[41]

His jottings for that crucial year indicate that he felt the die was cast: "The time for argument is past, the time for action is now come.... Our course I regard as now fixed."[42]

McCheyne had the support of the congregation at St. Peter's. In December 1842 the elders drew up a declaration backing the decisions reached at the convocation. They also declared their "unshaken attachment" to their pastor for "his abundant and devoted labours amongst us." He had been a blessing to many souls, "who shall be to him a crown of rejoicing in the day of the Lord." If McCheyne felt compelled to leave his position as minister, "the majority of his people as well as of the elders of this Congregation will feel themselves called upon to leave the Established Church along with him."[43] Sixteen min-

---

40. Brown, *Thomas Chalmers and the Godly Commonwealth*, 330–31; Burleigh, *Church History*, 350–51.

41. Andrew A. Bonar, *Memoir*, 146. McCheyne made copious notes in a small notebook on the sessions of the convocation. MACCH 1.16.

42. Cost of erecting church buildings, support of the ministry, 1839–1842, MACCH 1.15.

43. Declaration by the Elders of the Congregation and Parish of St. Peter's, Dundee, December 1842, MACCH 2.7.14. Declaration by the Elders of the Congregation and Parish of St. Peter's.

isters from Dundee Presbytery, including McCheyne, adhered to the resolutions of the convocation at Edinburgh. Six probationers were also in agreement.[44]

One of the last acts of McCheyne in the cause of Non-Intrusion was to chair a meeting in St. Peter's for the purpose of organizing the congregation to raise money on behalf of the Free Protesting Church, as disruption was now inevitable. Bonar commented that he spoke fervently at that meeting.[45]

## Burns's Timely Warning

At a time when contention over patronage and the spiritual independence of the church was gradually reaching a climax, William Chalmers Burns, already much used in revival, issued a timely warning. He sensed how, in the heat of contention for scriptural principles, it was possible for the individual to be diverted from experiencing a vital saving union with Christ. In an address given in Reverend A. Moody Stuart's church in Edinburgh on the eve of the Disruption, he referred to the woman at Sychar's well in Samaria (John 4). She would have been content to discuss the differences between the Jewish worship and her own. The Lord directed her to Himself and her great need of salvation. Burns continued:

> In times when important controversies agitate the land, men are constantly making them a shelter in which to escape direct personal drawing near to God in Christ. Thus we see, that when the Lord came to close dealing with this poor woman, she turned off his searching words by asking his judgment on the great controversy of that day. It is much to be feared that this is just what men are doing in Scotland now. They shift off all inquiry as to the state of their hearts and consciences, into the taking up of a side, and embracing of a principle: and though the principle be good, yet it is plain, that if this be all the length to which their religion goes, it cannot save them.

---

44. *List of Ministers who adhered to the resolution of the Convocation at Edinburgh, 22 November 1842* (Edinburgh: Peter Brown, 1843).

45. Andrew A. Bonar, *Memoir*, 162.

It is hard to see them holding fast a truth which condemns, while they let go a truth which might save them. For this truth they contend, that Christ is the King and only Head of his Church. But then, that is a truth in the order of God which grows out of this first truth, that Christ is the King and the Head of each man who believes.[46]

Having traced the troubled ecclesiastical background of those years, I will now consider the early years of McCheyne in Dundee.

---

46. William C. Burns, *Revival Sermons: Notes of Addresses*, ed. M. F. Barbour (Edinburgh: Banner of Truth Trust, 1980), 84–85. Sermon delivered on May 17, 1843.

# 3

# Breaking Up the Fallow Ground: McCheyne's Early Years in Dundee, Preparing for Revival

[McCheyne's] years in Dundee were the years at the heart of the transformation from county town and port into industrial city with global trading networks. Amidst the smell, the unclean air, the overcrowding tenements around St. Peter's, and the growing inequalities between rich and poor, he sought to bring the gospel to all.

—David Robertson, *Awakening: The Life and Ministry of Robert Murray McCheyne*

I return to what I said at first, that many are called but few are chosen. We this day call to every one of you. We have laid before you the reason why you should flee from the wrath to come—because of the mountains of sin that are lying on you. We have laid before you the completeness and all-sufficiency of Christ to bear all that load. And there is not one of you too cold, too hard, too careless that we despair of your conversion this day.

—Robert Murray McCheyne, sermon on Lydia and the jailer from Acts 16:12–36

The circular that emanated from St. John's Parish Church early in 1835, proposing the erection of a chapel in the northwest quarter of the Hawkhill, mentioned the need for a "pious, active, and efficient preacher." His task would be "to *excavate* a congregation for himself from the surrounding district."[1]

The St. John's kirk session had asked Dr. Chalmers, Dr. Welsh, and R. S. Candlish to suggest a list of six men suitable for the charge. The six included McCheyne and two of his close friends, Andrew Bonar and Alexander Somerville. Candlish believed McCheyne would be the best candidate for the work. McCheyne, however, thought otherwise. In a letter to his parents from Larbert, he wrote: "If the people have any sense they will choose Andrew Bonar, who for learning, experimental knowledge, and all the valuable qualities of a minister outstrips all the students I ever knew."[2] In August 1836 the congregation met to shorten the list but had already fixed on McCheyne in their minds. At the point of nomination, under the guiding hand of Roxburgh, one of those present, Simon Robertson, said several people wanted to know whether McCheyne read his sermons or not (a habit developed in the days of the Moderates). Roxburgh answered he did not. The motion to have McCheyne as minister "was carried by a great majority."[3]

His extempore preaching developed during his ten months as assistant minister at Larbert and Dunipace. Bonar recalled how one morning as McCheyne rode to Dunipace, his written sermons fell out of his saddle bags and were left on the wayside: "This accident prevented him having the opportunity of preparing in his usual manner; but he was enabled to preach with more than usual freedom. For the first time in his life, he discovered that he possessed the gift of extemporaneous composition, and learned to his own surprise, that he had more composedness of mind and command of language than he had believed. This discovery, however, did not in the least degree diminish his diligent preparation."[4] McCheyne came to St. Peter's with a strong testimonial from Reverend John Bonar of Larbert. He described his

1. Managers' Minutes of St. Peter's Church.

2. McCheyne to his parents, June 30, 1836, MACCH 2.6.32.

3. *Dundee, Perth, and Cupar Advertiser*, August 19, 1836; Van Valen, *Constrained by His Love*, 142–43.

4. Andrew A. Bonar, *Memoir*, 39.

assistant minister as a man of "excellent talents, solid study, sound principles and real piety." As to his character, he was "kindly and affectionate, modest and unassuming in manner," and his general deportment "altogether suitable to his profession." His preaching was "clear, distinct, pointed and impressive." Bonar concluded by saying: "He is greatly beloved and delighted in by my people.... I would count any parish highly privileged by having him appointed as their pastor."[5] Robertson summed up his assistant pastorate by saying Larbert was, in effect, the "finishing school" for McCheyne. He was well prepared through his visitation and preaching for the work he was to take up in Dundee.[6]

On November 2, 1836, three weeks before his ordination, McCheyne nailed his colors to the mast in a sermon preached before Dundee Presbytery. In speaking from Romans 2:28–29 in a sermon titled "Formality Not Christianity," he emphasized that external observances are of no avail to justify the sinner: "Remember, no outward observances, no prayers, or church going, or Bible-reading can ever justify you in the sight of God." He then addressed himself to the believers and warned how Satan, as an angel of light, continued to pursue the ordinances as the believer's all in all, instead of seeking growth in sanctification: "Pause, this hour, and see if, in your haste and anxious pursuit of the ordinances, you have not left the pursuit of that holiness without which the ordinances are sounding brass and a tinkling cymbal."[7] This was to be a recurring theme in later ministry.

The parish of St. Peter's had a population of four thousand souls, many of whom had no church connection. From the start St. Peter's, which could accommodate eleven hundred, was filled to capacity, though one-third of McCheyne's hearers came from distant parts of Dundee.[8] Bonar described it as a "very dead region." He maintained

---

5. Certificate from John Bonar, minister of Larbert and Dunipace, MACCH 2.6.28.

6. Robertson, *Awakening*, 64.

7. McCheyne, *From the Preacher's Heart*, 153–60.

8. Not only in St. Peter's but in other Dundee churches, McCheyne drew the crowds. He wrote to his parents and Willie on December 12, 1836: "In the evening I

that even those who were Christians were making no impact on the neighborhood. Rather, it was tending to deaden their faith. For himself, McCheyne saw he had his work cut out to make inroads on the area at all: "A city given to idolatry and hardness of heart. I fear there is much of what Isaiah speaks of: 'The prophets prophesy lies, and the people love to have it so.'"[9] A week after his ordination, he wrote to his parents and brother Willie of his impressions of Dundee in more detail. His first lodging was acceptable, "with the exception that it smokes a little. The reason probably is that there is so much smoke in the Dundee atmosphere, it cannot get up and therefore comes down to visit us." His estimate of his congregation showed that although he believed he would have an uphill task with them, echoing the sentiments of Bonar above, he was optimistic for the future:

> There is a fine flock of poor souls and when I can get the visiting set going I have little doubt I shall be enabled to keep up their attendance. I fear it is a very dark corner this. The light always appears to me like a single candle set in the midst of a dark church. It only makes the darkness visible. There seems even to be a kind of obscurity over the Christian people. They are infected by the surrounding mass.[10]

### His Impressions of the Spiritual State of Scotland

McCheyne's lectures on the seven churches of Asia, delivered in 1838, provide some insight as to how he saw the spiritual state of Scotland as a whole, and also the religious condition of Dundee. In the past travelers often compared Scotland to Philadelphia: it was a time "when every child could read the Bible; and when there was no need of Sabbath Schools, for every family was a Sabbath School. We are not

---

preached in the Old Church, a queer building with nooks and galleries around and about you. It was very much thronged even before the bells began so that it was only by dint of elbows and knees that I could make my way to the pulpit." MACCH 2.1.2.

9. Andrew A. Bonar, *Memoir*, 57.

10. McCheyne to his parents and Willie, November 30, 1836, MACCH 2.1.1. He hoped to find support from his kirk session when he met them: "The outward appearance of them is respectable. What they are inwardly I have yet to learn." MACCH 2.1.1.

a Philadelphia now, we are rather a Laodicea."[11] He applied the condition of Sardis to the spiritual state of Dundee:

> Although there are thousands in this place who have not even the name to live, who never enter the house of God, still there are many of you who come to church, who attend the prayer meeting, and you have a name to live, and yet you are dead. Where is the Christian who has living faith? Where is the Christian who has living love burning in his bosom to God? Where is the Christian who has living service, kind, affectionate, to the brethren?[12]

## McCheyne's Estimate of His Congregation

His lectures on the seven churches were delivered after he had a year or two to assess the state of his regular congregation. He felt that many of them fitted the description that the risen, ascended Christ gave of Laodicea:

> Who are the lukewarm? Those who have the form of godliness, but who deny the power thereof: those who are lovers of pleasure more than lovers of God; those who are faithful at ordinances, who come every Sabbath to church, who are faithful in the world, those who are almost persuaded to be Christians. Now, this is what Christ hates most of all—He would rather have you to be cold or hot, than to be lukewarm. Are there not some of you who mock at such a thing as warmth in religion, and call it enthusiasm, at having affection to Christ?[13]

McCheyne obviously felt that he had quite a mission field to labor in. He saw there was much ignorance of spiritual things, as well as indifference and hostility. In one of his sermons he remarked that thousands in Dundee turned away "with disgust from ministers and

---

11. McCheyne, *Brief Expositions*, 43–44.
12. McCheyne, *Brief Expositions*, 43–44.
13. McCheyne, *Brief Expositions*, 52.

sermons," without knowing the gospel message.[14] Those not accustomed to sitting under the preaching of an evangelical minister would, after a time, absent themselves from the house of God or go to hear "a less faithful minister where they may sit and live in sin."[15]

McCheyne was deeply conscious of the mixed congregation that normally attended his preaching. There were those who were in a state of grace but also many people still in their natural state and in their sins. In an address titled "The Wonder of Conversion," based on Zechariah 3:1–2 ("Is not this a brand plucked out of the fire?"), he said:

> This congregation is made up of these two: (1) Brands in the fire and (2) Brands plucked out of the fire. Have you never experienced a work of grace in your soul, never been convinced of sin nor drawn to Jesus? Then you are a brand in the fire. But there is one able to pluck you out. Oh, brands, cry upon Him. He alone is able and the time is short. Soon, soon you will be in the fire of hell out of which no hand can pluck you.[16]

In spite of the forthright and outspoken nature of his passionate preaching, McCheyne always had a packed church and a captive audience.

## Preparation of the Man: The Pursuit of Holiness and Self-Reformation

The title of this chapter is a reference to Hosea 10:12: "Break up your fallow ground: for it is time to seek the LORD."[17] Breaking up the fal-

---

14. McCheyne, *Passionate Preacher*, 314. His sermon was titled "The Record," on 1 John 5:11–12.

15. "When a lively minister of Christ comes to a town, the people often flock to hear for a little, but when they come to see the drift of the gospel—that it is a plan to turn them away from their sins—they soon drop away from the house of God or they seek a less faithful minister where they may sit and live in sin." McCheyne, *Passionate Preacher*, 277.

16. McCheyne, *Passionate Preacher*, 89.

17. Hosea 10:12: "Sow to yourselves in righteousness, reap in mercy; break up your fallow ground: for it is time to seek the LORD, till he come and rain righteousness upon you."

low ground has reference to heart preparation. "Fallow ground" is not wilderness; therefore, it cannot be applied to the unsaved. It is ground that in the past has yielded fruit but has become unproductive due to lack of cultivation—land that is lying idle. One of the greatest obstacles to revival is the vast tract of fallow ground in the hearts of professing Christians. Such hardened, tightly packed soil is God's way of describing believers who have grown insensitive to the way they grieve the Holy Spirit and are unresponsive to His still, small voice. It is hearts characterized by cold formality. Fallow ground is often weed covered, which would speak of failure to cultivate the soul diligently. It is essentially unfruitful ground, the words of Haggai 1:6 being applicable: "Ye have sown much, and bring in little." The fruit that God looks for in the Christian is Christlike character as set forth in Galatians 5:22–23: practical holiness in thought, word, and deed. It is clear, also, from the words "break up," that it is something the individual is exhorted to do. The responsibility for heart preparation lies with the Christian. To break up the fallow ground of our hearts means to bring them to a humble and contrite state before God, the only state God can begin to revive. Revival, therefore, begins at home.

One of the dominant characteristics of McCheyne's spiritual development is the way in which he himself took with great seriousness the constant need for growth in personal holiness and a closer walk with God. Yeaworth commented that "McCheyne's ministerial career was successful and effective only in so far as it reflected his own personal relationship to God."[18] The cultivation of his own soul was something he gave continuous attention to.

Two seventeenth-century divines had quite an influence on McCheyne. One was Richard Baxter (1615–1691), of whose writings he was fond.[19] In his *Reformed Pastor*, Baxter, taking as his text Acts 20:28, "Take heed therefore unto yourselves, and to all the flock," counseled as follows: "Content not yourselves with being in a state

---

18. David Victor Yeaworth, "Robert Murray McCheyne 1813–1843: A Study of an Early 19th Century Scottish Evangelical" (PhD diss., Edinburgh University, 1957), 95.

19. Robertson, *Awakening*, 58; and Andrew A. Bonar, *Memoir*, 26.

of grace, but be also careful that your graces are kept in vigorous and lively exercise, and that you preach to yourselves the sermons which you study, before you preach them to others. If you did this for your own sakes, it would not be lost labour."

He went on to state: "O brethren, watch therefore over your own hearts: keep out lusts and passions, and worldly inclinations; keep up the life of faith, and love, and zeal: be much at home, and be much with God."[20]

The other influence on McCheyne was Bishop Jeremy Taylor (1613–1667), who advocated to the ministers of his day: "If thou meanest to enlarge thy religion, do it rather by enlarging thine ordinary devotions than thy extraordinary."[21] Bonar commented that this statement epitomized the way in which McCheyne cultivated the development of his own soul. For, while he did from time to time set apart devotional seasons for special prayer and fasting, "the real secret of his soul's prosperity lay in the daily enlargement of his heart in fellowship with his God."[22]

That this continued on throughout his life is clear from the document titled "Reformation." An early version of this is in his diary, which begins March 27, 1839, and which even in the 1842 version was left unfinished, suggesting continual revision. [23] Personal reformation was the starting point, in harmony with Baxter's advice. He believed he would do most for God's glory and the good of men "by maintaining a conscience always washed in Christ's blood, by being filled with the Holy Spirit at all times, and by attaining the most entire likeness to Christ in mind, will, and heart, that is possible for a redeemed sinner to attain to in this world."

This would involve regular confession of sin in the widest possible sense at all times, especially on the Sabbath and during Communion seasons: "I ought to go to Christ for the forgiveness of each sin." It

20. Richard Baxter, *The Reformed Pastor*, ed. William Brown (London: Religious Tract Society, 1829), 31–32.
21. Andrew A. Bonar, *Memoir*, 54.
22. Andrew A. Bonar, *Memoir*, 54.
23. MACCH 1.8.

involved also being filled with the Spirit: striving for more purity, humility, meekness, patience under suffering, and love. "Make me Christ-like in all things should be my constant prayer. Fill me with the Holy Spirit."[24]

That McCheyne set a high standard for himself in his work as a minister is clear from an entry in one of his notebooks for the second year of his ministry. He asked the question, "What should a minister be?" and answered by giving an analysis of Paul's words in 1 Thessalonians 2. He had twenty-six points in all, beginning with boldness in preaching the gospel, which his extant sermons certainly show to have been the case. Then he emphasized the effort involved ("with much agony"), the trustworthy motives he should have, the pastoral heart and spirit he should employ, and the impeccable character that ought to mark a minister. These being adhered to, the fruit of his labors would be to see his spiritual children in glory at the coming of the Lord Jesus Christ.[25]

What characterized McCheyne then and shone through in his message was the holiness he pursued, which resulted from his constant emphasis on self-reformation. Van Valen highlighted this:

> The great secret of his proclamation is holiness! He not only practised, but also emphasized this aspect to a greater degree than most other teachers of the Scottish Church. Although he knew that many among God's children were not progressing in holiness, he never neglected to stress the point that holiness should be a reality in the Christian faith and life. Although he had to leave much room in his preaching for addressing the unconverted because of the spiritual condition of his audience, the stress on the need for holiness never fell into the background.[26]

His attention to personal self-reformation and holiness was noticed by others. His close friend Andrew Bonar noted in his diary

---

24. Andrew A. Bonar, *Memoir*, 149–56.

25. Sermons, 1837–1838, 1:170, MACCH 1.1; also in Smellie, *Robert Murray McCheyne*, 73–74.

26. Van Valen, *Constrained by His Love*, 477.

on March 19, 1837: "At Dundee for Robert McCheyne...I learned much from him especially and chiefly from his recollectedness of soul and nearness of communion with God. The attention of his people is remarkable, standing up, sometimes, in their eagerness."[27]

Because McCheyne's ministry consisted very much of "a bringing out of views that had first sanctified his own soul," therefore the "healthiness of his own soul was absolutely needful to the vigour and power of his ministration."[28] Those morning hours that were set apart for the nourishment of his own soul were therefore vital.[29]

### The Importance of Prayer and Prayer Meetings

After saying "break up your fallow ground," the prophet Hosea continues—"for it is time to seek the LORD." After heart preparation comes prevailing prayer. This was a matter of great importance to McCheyne. He took to heart the advice of Baxter: "Above all, be much in secret prayer and meditation. Hence you must fetch the heavenly fire that must kindle your sacrifices."[30] The second section of his personal reformation was "Reformation in Secret Prayer": "I ought not to omit any of the parts of prayer—confession, adoration, thanksgiving, petition, and intercession." To McCheyne it was important to begin the day with prayer, at least one hour alone with God, before seeing anyone. Then would come daily intercession for family, connections, relatives, friends, and his flock in great detail. He also interceded for missionaries to Jews and Gentiles.[31] Prayer was absolutely key to him: "I am persuaded that I ought never to do anything without prayer, and, if possible, special, secret prayer.... I ought to spend the best hours of the day in communion with God. It is my

---

27. Andrew A. Bonar, *Diary and Letters*, ed. Marjory Bonar (London: Hodder and Stoughton, 1893), 62.

28. Andrew A. Bonar, *Memoir*, 52.

29. "With him," wrote Bonar, "the commencement of all labour invariably consisted in the preparation of his own soul." *Memoir*, 34.

30. Baxter, *Reformed Pastor*, 32.

31. Andrew A. Bonar, *Memoir*, 156–57. See also Robertson, *Awakening*, 130–31, for an extended list of people and subjects prayed for.

noblest and most fruitful employment, and is not to be thrust into any corner."[32] McCheyne was never to appear before his people without much time spent in meditation and prayer, nor did he allow other legitimate duties to take precedence over such times. He was once asked whether parish duties on a Saturday interrupted his prayer life. To this he replied in the negative, adding, "What would my people do if I were not to pray?"[33] During his first years in Dundee, he often rode out in an afternoon to the ruined church at Invergowrie, on the outskirts of Dundee. There he enjoyed an hour of perfect solitude, where he could pray undisturbed.[34] Robertson comments that McCheyne's disciplined Bible reading and prayer life led to him knowing much of the presence of Christ and the power of God in his life.[35]

Shortly after being ordained, McCheyne began his weekly prayer meeting, the first of its kind in Dundee, on Thursdays. There was prayer to begin with, then a message from the pastor, then another time of prayer. As many as eight hundred people attended from different parts of the town. Accounts of past revivals were also read to them. These Thursday evening meetings had the effect, first of all, of strengthening the faith of believers.[36]

The faith of fellow evangelical ministers was also strengthened as, from time to time, those from nearby towns, such as Bonar from Collace or Macdonald from Blairgowrie, met together with McCheyne. They would spend a whole day "in confession of ministerial and personal sins, with prayer for grace, guiding ourselves by the reading of the Word." In the evening they would "unitedly pray for the Holy Spirit being poured down upon the people."[37]

---

32. Diary, 1839, MACCH 1.8; Andrew A. Bonar, *Memoir*, 158.
33. Andrew A. Bonar, *Memoir*, 52.
34. Andrew A. Bonar, *Memoir*, 56.
35. Robertson, *Awakening*, 132.
36. Andrew A. Bonar, *Memoir*, 62–63.
37. Andrew A. Bonar, *Memoir*, 71–72.

## Praying for Revival, Blessing Expected

Revival, indeed, was never far from McCheyne's thoughts. He expected it and prayed for God to work in revival power. Bonar noted that he expected a fruitful ministry.[38] He was also convinced that revival would begin with the people of God: "When God puts it into the hearts of his children to pray, it is certain that he is going to pour down his Spirit in abundance." God "pours water on 'him that is thirsty,' and then on the dry ground."[39] One reason why revival tarried, in McCheyne's opinion, was because the ministers themselves were not yet ready for it.[40] Nevertheless, he continued to believe God would work in their midst. Preaching July 1, 1838, on Isaiah 44:3–4, he said these words had often been in his heart and on his tongue since coming to Dundee:

> And yet, although God has never, from the very first day, left us without some tokens of his presence, he has never fulfilled this promise; and I have taken it up today, in order that we may consider it more fully, and plead it more anxiously with God.... Learn there is good hope of revival in our day. Learn that we should pray. We are often for preaching to awaken others; but we should be more concerned with prayer. Prayer is more powerful than preaching. It is prayer that gives preaching all its power.[41]

A few months earlier, when preaching on Christ's compassion on the multitudes, from Matthew 9:35–38, he said, "I have a sweet persuasion in my own breast, that if we go on in faith and prayer, building up God's altars that are desolate, God will hear the cry of His people and give them teachers according to his own heart; and that we shall yet see days such as have never before shone upon the Church of Scotland."[42]

---

38. Andrew A. Bonar, *Memoir*, 79.
39. Eighth pastoral letter, March 20, 1839, in Andrew A. Bonar, *Memoir*, 247–48.
40. Andrew A. Bonar, *Diary and Letters*, 41 (February 3, 1836).
41. McCheyne, *From the Preacher's Heart*, 82.
42. McCheyne, *From the Preacher's Heart*, 166. Preached at St. Peter's, November 12, 1837.

Taking as his text on one occasion Psalm 110:3, "Thy people shall be willing in the day of thy power," he referred to the Lord's words to Paul at Corinth, "For I have much people in this city," saying, "Ah, this is my hope speaking to you. If I thought that all Christ's people had been gathered out of this place I would leave you tomorrow to seek souls somewhere else."[43] McCheyne had great faith in the power of God to work, believing that the hardest of hearts would yield in the day of Christ's power. His certainty of this was remarked on by his contemporaries. Bonar noted in his diary: "From Robert McCheyne's conversation and preaching I observe the power God gives to strong faith."[44] What was necessary first, however, was that the congregation of St. Peter's should be set to work.

## Preparing the Flock: Involving the Whole Congregation in Church Work

The various meetings that took place in St. Peter's made it one of the busiest and most active congregations around. One of the elders, William Lamb, who became also Sabbath school superintendent, described St. Peter's as "a veritable bee-hive of industry when McCheyne was minister there," and the man himself an "indefatigable worker."[45] He inspired others, because he led by example. There was soon an active, working congregation. As well as the elders who carried out visitation in the districts assigned to them, there was a band of tract distributors who met periodically for prayer and Scripture reading before going out with the tracts. The Thursday meeting, begun soon after McCheyne's ordination, had the effect of quickening some of the believing Christians. To Bonar he wrote, "I give my people a Scripture to be hidden in the heart—generally a promise of the Spirit or the wonderful effects of His outpouring." He would then read some accounts of revival, with comments. People came from all parts of the

---

43. McCheyne, *Passionate Preacher*, 20.

44. Bonar, *Diary and Letters*, 59–60 (Saturday, December 30, 1837).

45. William Lamb, *McCheyne from the Pew: Being Extracts from the diary of William Lamb*, ed. Kirkwood Hewat (Stirling, Scotland: Drummond's Tract Depot, 1897), 95.

town to this meeting.[46] Both Lamb and McCheyne had an adult class. McCheyne described to his brother Willie how he conducted his:

> It is what I call the Geographical Method. I give them out some place such as "the Sea of Galilee," and bid them look up all the passages that refer to it in the Bible. Then I draw a map of it in chalk upon a board as we used to do at the High School. Then I teach them where all the places are. Then I read descriptions of it from Josephus the Jewish Historian, and from modern travellers.... Then I go over the places in the Bible which relate to it and illustrate them by the geographical positions and by the descriptions read. I find this very interesting to myself and they are quite delighted with it. There are 5 scenes on the Sea of Galilee described in the New Testament.[47]

McCheyne had a great love for young people. For them a Tuesday evening class was started, which attracted up to 250 young people. He led the meeting himself, using the Bible and catechism. Again, he sought to instill and retain interest by using his artistic ability to provide drawings to bring out the lessons. At times there would also be informal discussion. Bonar testified to the seriousness with which he took this work: "He thought himself bound to prepare diligently for his classes, that he might give accurate and simple explanations, and write what was interesting with the most solemn and awakening views."[48]

Great emphasis was laid on the children, and large Sabbath schools were set up, with an 8 a.m. meeting for children only on the Sabbath. Sabbath school itself was in the evening from 6 to 8 o'clock. In addition, day and evening schools were set up, the latter for girls who were working either as domestic servants during the day or in the factories. The Bible and catechism were taught, for McCheyne believed "the chief use of the school is to convert the souls of the children."[49]

---

46. Andrew A. Bonar, *Memoir*, 62–63.

47. McCheyne to his brother Willie, February 6, 1838, MACCH 2.1.35.

48. Andrew A. Bonar, *Memoir*, 60–61; Robertson, *Awakening*, 111.

49. Lamb, *McCheyne from the Pew*, 95–100; Van Valen, *Constrained by His Love*, 150–51.

Being musical and possessed of a good singing voice, McCheyne sought to improve the singing in St. Peter's. He held weekly meetings for singing practice. He must have set a high standard, for in 1841 the precentor, Mr. Renny, was dismissed from his post for the inefficient way in which he was conducting the psalmody.[50] Lamb commented that "all that went on made St. Peter's quite unique for the variety of its Christian enterprise and the number of its workers."[51]

## Visitation Work—A Vital Complement to Preaching

In addition to all the activities within St. Peter's, McCheyne was convinced of the need to go out to the people. Visitation was therefore an essential part of his work as a pastor. He saw it as complementing his preaching and teaching in St. Peter's. Here again, he took both the example and advice of Richard Baxter to heart. Baxter spent Mondays and Tuesdays, from morning to night, visiting fifteen or sixteen families in a week to try to cover his flock in a year.[52] In his *Reformed Pastor* he wrote, with regard to the importance of visitation: "I dare prognosticate from knowledge of the nature of true grace, that all godly ministers will make conscience of this duty, unless they be, by some extraordinary accident, disabled."[53] The words of McCheyne's old mentor, Chalmers, also remained with him. Chalmers practiced his own saying: "A house-going minister makes a church-going people."[54]

McCheyne's eyes were opened to the need for visitation when he had his first taste of it as a student. He recorded in his diary how he accompanied Andrew Bonar on one of his rounds in the Canongate area of Edinburgh, where he witnessed "depravity in all its forms."[55]

---

50. Meeting held in St. Peter's vestry, October 13, 1841, Managers' Minutes of St. Peter's Church.

51. Lamb, *McCheyne from the Pew*, 96.

52. Baxter, *Reformed Pastor*, 10.

53. Baxter, *Reformed Pastor*, 12.

54. As quoted in Iain H. Murray, *A Scottish Christian Heritage* (Edinburgh: Banner of Truth Trust, 2006), 328.

55. Andrew A. Bonar, *Memoir*, 24:

> March 3 [,1834]—Accompanied A.B. in one of his rounds through some of the most miserable habitations I ever beheld. Such scenes I

He became a regular visitor there, such was the lasting impression made on him. Once settled at Larbert and Dunipace, he pursued a vigorous, systematic visitation policy. He recorded names of those visited, numbers in households, their occupations, the response he got, and what he spoke on.[56] Once in Dundee, he continued his visitation "geographically"; that is, he visited the whole parish area assigned to him, not just members or adherents of St. Peter's.[57] Hence he found himself conversing with Catholics, Dissenters, Baptists, Episcopalians, Glassites, Methodists, and even members of the Chartist church. There were also many who went nowhere to church. With his aptitude for summing up people very quickly and frankly, McCheyne wrote in his notebook of one man, "7 June 1837. John Robertson. Curious clownish man. Member of no church. Sits in Relief [Church]. His wife queer [i.e., eccentric] willing like lady—no minister within their door for 30 years. Spoke with plainness and authority. Took it well."[58]

After visiting several houses, he would draw in his notebook a map of the area visited, which could be up to eighteen households. In the evening he would hold a meeting in one of the houses or in a green. For example, of those eighteen families visited in February 1837, the following summary was entered in his notebook: "Met them in the home of David Ritchie. Spoke on Paul's conversion at about an hour's length. Spoke as plainly as I could manage. All very attentive

---

never before dreamed of. Ah! Why am I such a stranger to the poor of my native town? I have passed their doors thousands of times; I have admired the huge black piles of building; with their lofty chimneys breaking the sun's rays—why have I never ventured within? How dwelleth the love of God in me? How cordial is the welcome even of the poorest and most loathsome to the voice of Christian sympathy! What imbedded masses of human beings are huddled together, unvisited by friend or minister! "No man careth for our souls" is written over every forehead.

56. Visitation notebook, 103–55, 301–76, MACCH 1.10.

57. There were approximately seven hundred members who had a fixed seat for which they paid a good deal less than in other churches. Those who could not find a pew would sit on chairs in the aisles and galleries or even on the steps of the pulpit. Van Valen, *Constrained by His Love*, 149.

58. Visitation notebook, 310, MACCH 1.10.

and interested.... Most shook hands very kindly."[59] He seemed to relish the regular visitation, regardless of whom he met. In a letter to his family in March 1837, he wrote, "I met great kindness in every house, though there were only 3 or 4 that belonged to my church. Most were old light dissenters, who have a great many truly godly people among them."[60] Follow-up work was often done by the elders, ten initially, four more being added in 1842. He wrote their names at the top of his notebook for the district for which they were responsible. They were also expected to bear the burden of Sunday school work, carrying out "an exacting supervision of the daily teaching."[61] These godly, dedicated men went a long way toward relieving the load of their pastor as much as possible. In addition, McCheyne introduced what he called "my system of Deaconesses," unordained, godly women who were given the responsibility of visiting the womenfolk.[62]

## Visitation of the Sick and Dying

McCheyne had a particular concern for the sick and dying, of whom there were many in Dundee at that time. A separate notebook was devoted in the main to such. Bonar recalled how he came to show such a strong interest in those who might never be fit to enter a church building again: "On another occasion, during the first year of his ministry [in Dundee], he witnessed the death-bed conversion of a man who, till within a few days of his end, almost denied that there was a God. This solid conversion, as he believed it to be, stirred him up to speak with all hopefulness, as well as earnestness, to the dying."[63] He revisited the sick repeatedly. Jean Ogilvie was visited from March 7 to November 22, 1838. At the end he noted: "Laid on

---

59. Visitation notebook, 305, MACCH 1.10.

60. McCheyne to Papa, Mamma, Eliza, and Willie, March 22, 1837, MACCH 2.1.11. Old Lights held to the Establishment principle that the civil magistrate had a power in matters of religion.

61. Van Valen, *Constrained by His Love*, 189; Robertson, *Awakening*, 107.

62. McCheyne to Papa, Mamma, Eliza, and Willie, March 13, 1837, MACCH 2.1.11: "I have employed Miss Carnegie to visit my poor Catholic Irish woman. My system of Deaconesses will work well."

63. Andrew A. Bonar, *Memoir*, 57–58.

her back now. Spoke plainly to her. I do hope Jean has a saving hold—
'The greatest sinner needs the hardest grip of Christ,' she told me."[64]
In some cases he was more confident of the spiritual state of those he
visited. Right at the start of his time in Dundee he visited Margaret
Low and devoted a whole page to several visits:

> Asked me to open the 89th Psalm which I did. She seems to
> know the name of the Savior. To her He is precious. Visited 8
> Dec. Asked me to open the 23rd Psalm which I did fully. She
> relishing Christ very plainly. On "my shepherd" she said "yes
> all the comfort is in his being ours. It would be nothing if he
> were only the shepherd of others." For his name's sake "yes the
> glory is his for he is worthy of it!"[65]

## Sabbath Preaching

It was the preaching on the Sabbath, however, that drew the largest
crowds. The impact of McCheyne's services was "soon felt throughout the town," with people coming from all parts of Dundee.[66] Lamb
noted that McCheyne was skillful in the selection of his texts, as
well as in the exposition of them; how he "sought to find acceptable words," which might be as "goads" and "nails" to stimulate and
strengthen his audience.[67] He had also come to recognize the value of
careful divisions of a sermon, "for nothing is more needful in making a sermon memorable and impressive than a logical argument."
His extant fleshed-out sermons illustrate this.[68] Although he had his
favorite portions of Scripture, such as the Song of Solomon, he ranged
freely around both Testaments. The Old Testament was for him a rich
field for his studies, "where he found the Gospel everywhere in type
and symbol."[69]

---

64. Dundee visitation, MACCH 1.14, 18.

65. Dundee visitation, MACCH 1.14, 1.

66. Andrew A. Bonar, *Memoir*, 63.

67. Lamb, *McCheyne from the Pew*, 39.

68. Murray, *Scottish Christian Heritage*, 317–18. He had earlier neglected to follow the rules his college tutor, Dr. Welsh, had laid down for dividing up a sermon.

69. Lamb, *McCheyne from the Pew*, 48. See also *Passionate Preacher*, 90–120, for
twenty different types of the Lord Jesus.

As to the content of his preaching, all the doctrines of grace, as embodied in the Scots Confession of Faith, were preached. For example, in his estimation, justification by faith alone in the finished work of Christ was a foundational doctrine that could never be neglected. In his introductory comments on Galatians in his annotated *Bagster's Bible*, he quoted Luther on the matter of righteousness and justification—"If the article of justification be once lost then is all true Christian doctrine lost," commenting, "And as many as are in the work that hold not the doctrine are either Jews, Turks, Papists or Heretics. For between the righteousness of the law and Christian righteousness there is no mean—he then that strayeth from this Christian righteousness must needs fall into the righteousness of the law."[70] McCheyne laid great emphasis on ruin by the fall, the depravity of man, and the full redemption that is in Christ Jesus. Where he differed from others, however, and especially from the Moderates even within the presbytery, was in this: he not only preached the doctrines of Scripture, and there was usually a great deal of biblical truth in his messages, but he also preached Christ, "from whom all doctrine shoots forth as rays from a centre."[71]

To McCheyne, there was no inconsistency in preaching the doctrine of God's sovereign electing grace and making a free offer of the gospel to whosoever will. For example, in a sermon on electing love from John 15:16 ("Ye have not chosen me, but I have chosen you") he said, "Let me take up the truths in this verse as they occur." The first was "Men naturally do not choose Christ.... Brethren, the truth here taught us is this, that every awakened sinner is willing to embrace Christ, but not till made willing." He then moved to his second head, that Christ chooses His own disciples: "Everyone whom he brings to glory, he chooses." It was a choice that could be traced back into eternity, said McCheyne, as he referred to 2 Thessalonians 2:13

---

70. *Bagster's Bible* (London: Samuel Bagster, 1828), 2: introduction to Galatians, Dundee City Archives.

71. Andrew A. Bonar, *Memoir*, 65.

and Ephesians 1:4. The reason for His choice was the good pleasure of His will.[72]

Notice, however, his passionate entreaty to St. Peter's congregation on John 7:37 ("In the last day, that great day of the feast, Jesus stood and cried"):

> Observe, it was when the whole people of the land were met together that Jesus stood and cried: "If any man thirst, let him come unto me and drink."... When thousands came together, Jesus would not miss the happy opportunity: "Jesus stood and cried." O my friends! Jesus still stands in the crowded assembly. May you hear his voice this day!... I doubt not there were many a Jew there that day who never heard the voice of the Savior again and therefore I can see what was in the mind of Christ when he lifted up his voice so loud: "Jesus stood and cried!" There may be some here today that will never hear the word of Christ again. This may be the last day of the feast to some of you. Oh! then, that we might stand and cry—lift up the voice like a trumpet, and say: "If any man thirst, let him come unto me and drink!"; and O that you would hear as for eternity!... O thirsty souls—afflicted, tempest-tossed, and not comforted—why will ye not come unto Jesus, the smitten rock, to drink?[73]

In another sermon, "Melting the Betrayer," on John 13:21 ("one of you shall betray me"), he shows how repeatedly the Lord Jesus, who knew Judas's heart and yet loved him, sought to win him from his intended betrayal. He then confronted his congregation with these words: "There is not within these walls one of you so hard, so cold, so base, so unmoved, so far from grace and godliness, so Judas-like, that Jesus does not grieve over your hardness, that you will still resist all his love, that you will still love death, and wrong your own soul."[74]

---

72. R. M. McCheyne, *Basket of Fragments* (Inverness: Christian Focus, 1979), 94–102.

73. McCheyne, *From the Preacher's Heart*, 301–5.

74. McCheyne, *From the Preacher's Heart*, 61–69.

McCheyne never sought to make the way of salvation easy in order to make it plain. As he preached on Matthew 11:28, "Come unto me," he said:

> As far as the Lord has given me light in this matter, and look-ing at what my own heart does in like circumstances, I do not feel that there is anything more in coming to Jesus, than just believing what God says about His Son to be true. I believe that many people keep themselves in darkness by expecting something more than this. Some of you will ask, 'Is there no appropriating of Christ? No putting out of the hand of faith? No touching the hem of his garment?' I quite grant, beloved, there is such a thing, but I do think it is inseparable from believing the record. If the Lord persuades you of the glory and power of Immanuel, I feel persuaded that you cannot but choose Him.[75]

Because he was always afraid of superficial conversion, he laid great emphasis on the depravity of human nature: "You must see yourself a vile, lost sinner and Christ a full free Savior, else you cannot enter in at the straight gate."[76] In his counseling also, whether one-on-one or by correspondence, he sought to bring inquirers to realize how lost they were, for to him this was the first work of the Holy Spirit in bringing a soul to Christ. To one soul seeking Christ, he wrote:

> Oh, pray for deep discoveries of your real state by nature and by practice! The world will say you are an innocent and harm-less girl: do not believe them…. Pray to see yourself exactly as God sees you; pray to know the worth of your own soul. Have you seen yourself as vile, as Job saw himself? Have you experienced anything like Psalm 51? Perhaps you will ask, why

---

75. Andrew A. Bonar, *Memoir*, 78. When one lady came to him, assenting to his gospel message yet refusing to be comforted, McCheyne, always looking upon com-ing to Christ as something in addition to really believing the record God has given of His Son, reminded her of John 3:16–17. The woman said God did not care for her, at which he "convicted her of making God a liar; and, as she went away in great distress, his prayer was, 'Lord give her light.'" *Memoir*, 80.

76. McCheyne, *Passionate Preacher*, 142–43.

do you wish me to have such a discovery of my lost condition? I answer, that you may be broken off from all schemes of self-righteousness.[77]

## Preaching to a Mixed Congregation

McCheyne always preached to a mixed company from different backgrounds. In the past, some people would have sat under a Moderate ministry. Others might well have felt the influence of Sandemanianism.[78] To Sandemanians, the "heart" was the mind. Sandemanians were concerned to safeguard justification by faith. The only way they saw to do this was to say faith was something solely in the intellect. In doing so they reduced saving faith to an intellectual assent to the truths of the gospel.[79] By contrast, McCheyne followed closely the Westminster Confession, with its stress on the "trust of the heart." Like Whitefield, he preached a "felt Christ." Unbelief to him was always due to the state of the heart.

McCheyne, therefore, so structured his messages that there was something for the unawakened, the awakened, and also those who had come to Christ. A few months after arriving in Dundee, he spoke on John 16:8, "And when he is come, he will reprove the world." After opening up the subject of righteousness and conviction thereof, he said to the unawakened: "See how far you are from salvation.... You are as far from salvation as any one can be that is in the land of the living. The Spirit must convince you of Christ's righteousness." Then

---

77. Andrew A. Bonar, *Memoir*, 296–97.

78. The roots of Sandemanianism are found in the views of John Glas (Robert Sandeman's father-in-law). Glas's teaching was "fitted to put a premium upon what is held to be orthodox doctrine, and to lay less stress than is called for on the reaction of the emotional nature to the truth of the gospel, and on the activity of the will as that goes out in the trust of the heart and its attendant obedience in the life." The three men associated with Sandemanianism are John Glas, Robert Sandeman, and Archibald Maclean. D. M. Lloyd-Jones, *The Puritans: Their Origins and Successors* (Edinburgh: Banner of Truth Trust, 1987), 171–73; See also *Cyclopedia of Biblical, Theological, and Ecclesiastical Literature*, ed. John McClintock and James Strong (Grand Rapids: Baker, 1981), 9:337.

79. Lloyd-Jones, *Puritans*, 174–75, 176.

he addressed the awakened, by which he meant those who had come to a realization of their misery by means of the law, yet still required the Spirit's work to lead them to Christ: "Many are convinced who are never converted. Many are now in hell who were once as anxious to escape as you.... Cry night and day that he [God] would reveal Christ unto you—that he would shine into your darkness, and give you the light of the knowledge of the glory of God in the face of Jesus Christ." Then he had a word for those who had come to Christ. He spoke of them as miracles of grace, once loathsome but now led to embrace Christ. "O to grace how great a debtor!... Will you not love him with all your heart? Will you not serve him with all you have?"[80]

In that same year he preached a searching message on Genesis 19:26, Lot's wife becoming a pillar of salt. He saw her as a type of one convinced yet never converted: "She was really alarmed, and really fled; and yet her terrors were like the morning cloud and the early dew, which quickly pass away." But—"Her sons-in-law, her friends, her house, her goods, her treasure were still in Sodom; so her heart was there also.... So it is with many among us. Many flee under terrors of natural conscience, but when these subside, they look back and are lost." His main lesson was, "Learn that an awakening by mere natural conscience is very different from an awakening by the Spirit of God. No man ever fled to Christ from mere natural terror." He went on to show how she was helped to flee: "Some are laid hold of by God and made to flee, who yet look back and are lost. She was drawn out by angels (vs. 16). Grace did something for her, but it did not do everything. She was awakened yet never saved. An awakened soul is not a saved soul. You are not saved till God has shut you into Christ."[81]

What grieved McCheyne deeply was to observe a packed congregation, with many coming regularly to sit under his ministry yet remaining unmoved. This had led him, while still at Larbert, to speak of the danger of becoming gospel hardened. Preaching on Proverbs

---

80. McCheyne, *Passionate Preacher*, 317–28, the second of two sermons on this text, preached at St. Peter's in February 1837.

81. McCheyne, *From the Preacher's Heart*, 249–57.

1:20–23, "Turn you at my reproof," he expressed his fears for those who would not turn:

> The tenderness of a Saviour's love, if resisted then, will every day lose more of its novelty and of its power to touch the heart, the habit of resistance to the word and testimony of a beseeching God will every day become more predominant, the stony heart will every day become more adamant, the triple brass of unbelief will every day become more impenetrable. Oh! my friends, it is fearful to think how many among us are every hour subjecting our hearts to this sure and silent process of hardening. Oh! it is the saddest of all sights that a godly minister can behold to see his flock, Sabbath after Sabbath, waiting most faithfully on the stirring ministrations of the Word, and yet going away unawakened and unimpressed; for well he knows that the heart that is not turned is all the more hardened.[82]

## Preparation for Communion Services

McCheyne was also deeply exercised, because of his mixed congregation, to ensure that necessary instruction and discipline[83] were administered over his flock, particularly with regard to being allowed to take Communion. He had increased the number of Communion seasons from two a year to four.[84] He introduced his communicant

---

82. McCheyne, *From the Preacher's Heart*, 26–27 (full sermon, 21–29). This sermon was preached at Larbert, November 15, 1835, and no doubt on other occasions also.

83. When he began his ministry, he did not see the value of discipline, being happy to leave it to others. When, however, he observed that some souls were converted through "the key of discipline," a "new light broke in upon my mind." Thereafter it was of prime importance to him. Similarly, with regard to the matter of baptism, McCheyne was reluctant to baptize children of ungodly, unbelieving parents, insisting that water did not save a soul. When asked on such occasions, he seized the opportunity to remonstrate with them about the state of their own souls. Andrew A. Bonar, *Memoir*, 72–73.

84. There were several services held. There was an ante-sacramental sermon the Sabbath before Communion. Then, on the following Thursday were held two Fast Day services to get people in the correct spiritual frame. On the Friday and Saturday before, there were preparatory services, and on the Monday following Communion,

classes, not at all common in Scotland at that time, before his first Communion in Dundee. Many had come to Communion in the past without any form of examination or self-scrutiny. These classes were to prove a fruitful time, when he got to know individual members of his congregation well. The close-quarters challenging of individuals, who might sit through a sermon in a packed auditorium unmoved, brought many under conviction and some to faith in Christ. Sometimes he would host communicants at the manse in a group. He wrote to his family in April 1837 of feeling tired after having thirty guests: "Some of my communicants seem very deeply interested, and some give good reason to think that they are truly converted."[85]

His tract "This Do in Remembrance of Me," published in 1840 but in use before that date, gives us an indication of how he viewed many candidates. In the second paragraph he wrote pointedly and bluntly:

> I fear the Lord's Supper is profaned in a dreadful manner among you. Many come who are living in positive sins, or in the neglect of positive duties. Many come who know that they were never converted. Many who in their hearts ridicule the very thoughts of conversion. Unworthy communicating is a fearful sin; on account of it God is greatly provoked to withdraw His Spirit from you, to visit you with frowns of providence, and to seal you to the day of perdition.[86]

---

a thanksgiving service. On the actual Communion Sunday, "the great feast day," the partaking could last up to seven hours, even with several ministers assisting at the "sittings." An action sermon, with a fencing of the table, was delivered just prior to partaking. Lamb, *McCheyne from the Pew*, 70; Van Valen, *Constrained by His Love*, 228–29.

85. McCheyne to Papa, Mamma, and Willie, April 20, 1837, MACCH 2.1.13.

86. Andrew A. Bonar, *Memoir*, 569. He let them know that he was not taken in by their "serious face and air," and because they would "sit down, and look deeply solemnised," taking the bread into their hands, "pretending to declare that you have been converted.... Are you not afraid lest, while you are sitting at the Table, you should hear the voice of the Lord Jesus saying, 'Judas, betrayest thou the Son of Man with a kiss?'" Andrew A. Bonar, *Memoir*, 575.

The extent of this problem can be seen in the forceful comments in many of his extant sermons that include "fencing the tables"[87] as Communion season approached. In a sermon on 1 Corinthians 3:10, "As a wise masterbuilder, I have laid the foundation," he said: "I would have you briefly examine whether you have been rightly built upon the one foundation.... We do not know your hearts. We judge by your life, by your knowledge and by your experience, but God judges by the heart.... Do not be satisfied that a minister has admitted you."[88]

## Preparation for Revival: Evident Signs of Spiritual Life

It remains to be asked what impact McCheyne and his band of hardworking helpers had in those first few years on the congregation he had been required to "excavate." First, the people would have noticed the consistency of his daily walk with God. Once again, he appears to have taken to heart the advice of Richard Baxter, to the effect it was not sufficient to do all the preparation and preach well: "He that means as he speaks, will surely do as he speaks. One proud, surly, lordly word, one needless contention, one covetous action, may cut the throat of many a sermon, and blast the fruit of all that you have been doing."[89]

McCheyne conducted himself as always in the presence of God, whether out walking, riding, or distributing tracts and whether in conversation or in company with others, when he would try to turn the conversation to the things of eternity. His deep love for the Lord could not be hid. From that flowed his love for saint and sinner alike. He was never deterred by the opposition of cold-hearted ministers, nor did he allow his zeal for the Lord's work to be affected in any

---

87. *Cyclopedia of Biblical, Theological, and Ecclesiastical Literature*, 3:529: Fencing the tables is "a special address in the ministration of the Lord's Supper among Scotch Presbyterians. It is a lecture from the minister just before the distribution of the elements, pointing out the character of those who have and those who have not a right to come to the Lord's Table. It was formerly called 'debarrings,' as it debarred from the sacrament those who were not supposed to be worthy."

88. McCheyne, *Passionate Preacher*, 187.

89. Baxter, *Reformed Pastor*, 33–34.

way.[90] The townsfolk sensed there was a "peculiar man of God" in their midst. The tone of Christians was being raised "as much by his holy walk as by his heavenly ministry."[91]

Second, McCheyne had a very optimistic spiritual outlook. He fully expected, as already noted, that the Lord would bless a faithful ministry. To his father he wrote in June 1837, "There is an awakening look about my people and I really fear I dare not leave them."[92]

Third, his preaching on the Sabbath, which drew the largest congregation, attracted people from all parts of Dundee and beyond. Many people began to travel long distances to hear McCheyne, some coming from country parishes where they had sat under the ministry of Moderates. It was said of such that they "would return home with their hearts burning, as they talked of what they had heard that day."[93] Bonar recalled how "the Lord began to work by his means almost from the first day he came. There was ever one and another stricken, and going apart to weep alone."[94]

Fourth, the references in his diary for those early years indicate that his communicants' class was proving a fruitful field. Communion seasons were a time of both conviction and blessing. He recorded the following at the time of a spring Communion:

> These were happy days. Mr. D was awakened by coming to the communicants' class. Another by the action sermon. At the words, "I know thee, Judas," she trembled, and would have risen from the Table. These were glad days when one and another was awakened. The people looked very stirred and anxious, every day coming to hear the words of eternal life,—some inquiring in private every week.... About fifteen cases came to my knowledge the first sacrament.... Several

---

90. Andrew A. Bonar, *Memoir*, 82–83.

91. Andrew A. Bonar, *Memoir*, 82–83.

92. McCheyne to Papa, on the occasion of being asked to consider a call to St. Martin's, Perth, June 19, 1837, MACCH 2.1.17.

93. Andrew A. Bonar, *Memoir*, 66.

94. Andrew A. Bonar, *Memoir*, 67.

Christians seemed quickened to greater joy, and greater love one to another.[95]

Fifth, as well as preaching, McCheyne kept open house (or manse) for counseling seekers. This was a weekly occurrence. On one occasion two youngsters wrote to him desiring to speak, "for we are anxious about our souls." Others who came had previously been hardened against the gospel, or refused tracts offered to them. Some had made a false profession while others were open sinners. "In short, the Lord glorified Himself by the variety of those whom His grace subdued, and the variety of means by which His grace reached its object."[96]

In McCheyne's first few years in Dundee, therefore, there were obvious tokens of a town showing some evidence of God's visitation. These were, however, but mercy drops compared to the outpouring that was soon to come.

## Worn Out and Preparing to Leave for Palestine

Ill health and overwork forced McCheyne's retiral to Edinburgh toward the end of 1838. This may have been brought on by the occasion when he fell from a horizontal bar and lost consciousness for a time.[97] Nevertheless, he kept in touch with his flock, something his friend Andrew Nielson advised him to do. He suggested writing pastoral letters "not only to delight but also edify the flock." These could be read to his Thursday evening meetings, "compensating in some

---

95. Andrew A. Bonar, *Memoir*, 81. He gave a retrospective account of awakenings in a diary entry for March 1838: "The first success among my people was at the time of my first sacrament: then it appeared. My first sermon on Isaiah 61, 1 was blessed to _____ and some others. That on Ezek. 22, 14 'Can thine heart endure,' etc was blessed to awaken M.L. That on Song v, 2 'Open to me,' etc the Sabbath after the Sacrament, was blessed to another. M.D. was awakened by coming to the communicants' class. Another by the action sermon." *Memoir*, 80–81.

96. Andrew A. Bonar, *Memoir*, 79.

97. Robertson favors the view of Thomas Guthrie, that McCheyne's fall from the bar he had erected in James Grierson's garden for Grierson's son was the start of all his physical complaints from then on. Robertson, *Awakening*, 144; Van Valen, *Constrained by His Love*, 252–53.

measure for [his] absence." It was during his enforced absence from them that the deep bond of love and affection which existed between pastor and flock became increasingly evident. A congregational prayer meeting was started specifically for his recovery.[98] Six members of the congregation wrote to McCheyne in March 1839 to let him know of their daily prayers for his recovery. They added, "We have much reason to thank God that he ever sent you in the midst of us, and God has blessed your ministry much already." They concluded by thanking God they had a praying pastor, "to hold up our needy case to Him who knows the hearts of all men."[99] Not long before he departed for his Palestine trip, two others, Stewart Barnett and Eliza McLaren, in a letter of gratitude for his ministry, wrote, "Oh, that it may please the wise disposer of all events to restore you to your wonted health and your disconsolate congregation, will ever be the earnest and constant prayer of your devoted servants."[100]

The prayer meetings appeared to be addressing the lack of integration between the social classes, which George Lewis wrote of (see chapter 1). One working-class member of the congregation wrote to McCheyne with obvious surprise and delight at the way a "rich elder" had invited her small house prayer group to "join one in the school room appointed by the elders for our ministers." Her comment was, "Our weekly prayer meeting never was so well filled as it is now."[101]

It is tribute to his humility and submission to the ways of God that McCheyne believed being removed from his sphere of labor had two purposes: he would not be able to say "My hand and my eloquence have done it!" and all glory would be given to God: "May it really be so with my dear people!"[102] His optimistic spirit remained, as his eighth pastoral letter, penned just before leaving Edinburgh,

---

98. Mrs. Low to McCheyne, February 6, 1839, MACCH 2.1.58: "Your people have set apart a night in the week to pray for your recovery."

99. Alexander Fleming and five others to McCheyne, March 4, 1839, MACCH 2.1.63.

100. Stewart Barnett and Eliza McLaren to McCheyne, March 18, 1839, MACCH 2.1.71.

101. Mrs. Likely to McCheyne, January 29, 1839, MACCH 2.1.51.

102. Andrew A. Bonar, *Memoir*, 85.

revealed. He urged his flock on to greater prayer efforts: "When God gives grace to souls, it is in answer to the prayers of His children.... When God puts it into the hearts of His children to pray, it is certain that He is going to pour down His Spirit in abundance.... Ye that are the Lord's remembrancers, keep not silence, and give Him no rest."[103]

When, at the prompting of Dr. Candlish, McCheyne welcomed the opportunity to go with Andrew Bonar; Dr. Black of Marischal College and University, Aberdeen; and Dr. Keith of St. Cyrus Parish on a mission of inquiry to Palestine, he sought guidance from the Lord for a temporary replacement. The answer to prayer came in the person of William Chalmers Burns, son of the minister of Kilsyth. The elders of St. Peter's wrote to McCheyne, expressing their gratitude for "one whose qualifications are so highly spoken of.... They would offer him all the support and encouragement in their power."[104] McCheyne wrote to Burns that he was given in answer to prayer: "And these gifts are, I believe, always without exception blessed. I hope you may be a thousand times more blessed among them than ever I was. Perhaps there are many souls that would never have been saved under my ministry, who may be touched under yours; and God has taken this method of bringing you into my place. His name is wonderful."[105]

Because of his own attention to self-reformation, McCheyne was well qualified to give the following advice to Burns, on his accepting pulpit supply, which was to start on the first week of April:

> Take heed to *thyself*. Your own soul is your first and greatest care. You know a sound body alone can work with power; much more a *healthy soul*. Keep a clean conscience through the blood of the Lamb: keep up close communion with God. Study likeness to Him in all things. Read the Bible for your own growth first, then for your people.... Be of good courage; there remaineth much of the land to be possessed. Be not dismayed, for Christ shall be with thee to deliver thee.

---

103. Andrew A. Bonar, *Memoir*, 247–48.
104. Elders of St. Peter's to McCheyne, March 11, 1839, MACCH 2.1.67. There are twenty-five signatories, fifteen of them signed "elder."
105. Andrew A. Bonar, *Memoir*, 88–89.

# 4

# "That Memorable Field":
# Burns's Seven Months in Dundee

The officiating minister, Mr. Burns, is occupied during the early part of the day in examining and conversing with catechumens; and he is assisted in the evening exercises by other ministers...by the Reverend Messrs Baxter of Hilltown, Stewart of Lochee, Hamilton of Abernyte, Murray of Aberdeen, Bonar of Kelso, Reid of Chapelshade etc.... His countenance indicates great fervour of feeling and firmness of purpose— his manner and elocution are quite natural and unaffected. When he opens his address he appears diffident almost to hesitation; but as he proceeds, his voice acquires depth and pathos, and he occasionally rises to a high pitch of fervid and empassioned eloquence. In such passages he seems to exert great power over his audience; and, although he sometimes violates the rules of strict taste, yet he has great fluency of diction and facility of illustration, with a ready command of appropriate language and imagery. Some will be offended with his sentiments, and others with the severity of the terms in which they are conveyed, but no one can listen to him for any length of time without feeling in the presence of one gifted with no ordinary powers. In fact, the crowds that attend his evening discourses, and hang for hours upon his accents, are a proof that there is no common attraction in the speaker.

—*Dundee, Perth, and Cupar Advertiser*,
Friday, August 23, 1839

No sooner had William Chalmers Burns entered into the assurance of salvation in January 1832 than he felt the call to preach the gospel.[1] It was a full seven years later, however, before he was licensed to preach by the Presbytery of Glasgow.[2] In the intervening years he became increasingly exercised to preach the gospel abroad. It was while he was in the midst of communications with different committees regarding this that he wrote, "Mr McCheyne, about to set out for Palestine, wrote, asking me to take his place at Dundee. I found myself unexpectedly free to do this, and being speedily licensed I entered on my duties in that memorable field."[3] Still with an eye to the foreign field and bearing in mind his lack of pastoral experience, he replied to McCheyne that "it will not be a little beneficial especially with reference to my ultimate desires, to have an opportunity so favourable of making proof of my ministry of Christ among my dear countrymen."[4]

## Two Features of Burns's Spiritual Life

As he entered upon his temporary pastorate at Dundee in April 1839, Burns was a young licentiate, just turned twenty-four years of age. Though young in years, there were two features of his spiritual life that were to stand him in good stead for the task which lay ahead. First, Burns retained throughout his life a strong sense of his own unworthiness and insufficiency to accomplish anything by himself. This led him to be completely dependent on God at all times. Second, he had already developed a deep prayer life. Islay Burns, his younger brother by two years, recorded how one contemporary writer in the *Sunday at Home*, a family magazine for Sabbath reading, described him: "Above all, Mr Burns was a man of prayer. No one could be long in his company without discovering that. All the week long 'he filled the fountains of his spirit with prayer,' and on Sabbath the full fountain gave forth its abundant treasures. There was a freshness, a

---

1. McMullen, *God's Polished Arrow*, 21.
2. McMullen, *God's Polished Arrow*, 21; and Islay Burns, *Memoir of the Rev. William Chalmers Burns*, 53.
3. McMullen, *God's Polished Arrow*, 23.
4. Burns to McCheyne, March 2, 1839, in McMullen, *God's Polished Arrow*, 262.

simplicity, a scriptural force and directness in his prayers, that formed the best of all preparations for the discourse that was to follow."[5]

Islay Burns's own estimate of his brother was that "his whole life was literally a life of prayer, and his whole ministry a series of battles fought at the mercy-seat."[6]

One who knew him well at the start of his time in Dundee described how his host, Mr. P. H. Thoms, showed him around the parish and visited a few homes with him. On returning home, Burns went to his room to agonize before the Lord:

> He had gotten such an overwhelming sense of his responsi-
> bility for the souls of that people, that he could then think of
> nothing else.... We did not see him again till late in the eve-
> ning, when he came for the family worship. His prayer then
> was one continued strain of self-loathing, and pleading for
> mercy through "the blood of the Lamb of God." It happened
> that his room was next to mine, and *all that night* I heard him
> still groaning in prayer.[7]

Less than a year later, Andrew Bonar noted in his diary: "The lesson God is teaching me is this, that William Burns is used as the instrument where others have been labouring in vain, because he is much in prayer, beyond all of us. It is not the peculiar words he uses that God blesses."[8]

## St. Peter's on Burns's Arrival

Soon after his arrival, Burns wrote to his sister Jane that he had entered a ground well prepared for the gospel, with "not a few" hearts prepared to listen to God's Word. He found some to be quite well advanced in the spiritual life, which would "afford the strongest stim-ulus to my own growth in grace." At the same time, he questioned

---

5. Islay Burns, *Memoir*, 544–45.
6. Islay Burns, *Memoir*, 545.
7. Islay Burns, *Memoir*, 545–46n1.
8. Andrew A. Bonar, *Diary and Letters*, 85 (Monday, February 3, 1840). In his own journal for April 4, 1839, Burns wrote, "O for a spirit of humble wrestling prayer for the outpouring of his Spirit." McMullen, *God's Polished Arrow*, 31.

whether the congregation would regard him as filling McCheyne's pulpit adequately, or "as an ignorant babbler."[9] He was more explicit in a retrospective letter to McCheyne as he was about to relinquish his temporary pastorate. He found "that the necessity of union to Jesus, and entire dedication to his service and his glory, was a truth to which the mind of the congregation in general had been brought under your ministry to yield assent, and one which, through the mighty power of the Holy Spirit, not a few seemed to have savingly realized in their consciences and hearts."[10]

What appalled him was that many were unconcerned about their souls: "There were hundreds in the congregation and parish who, with a name to live, were in reality 'dead in trespasses and sins.'"[11]

## Continuing with the Work McCheyne Began

Burns's time in Dundee divided clearly into two parts, before and after his visit to Kilsyth in early July. In those early months, as he wrote to McCheyne later, he enjoyed much of the Lord's presence in his own soul. He was laying by "stores of divine knowledge" that would stand him in good stead for the various services he had to take at St. Peter's.[12] He also set himself to continue the thorough pastoral work that McCheyne had begun. Like McCheyne, he took time to visit the sick. For example, he recorded in his journal for Fast Day, April 18, how he visited twelve-year-old James Wallace "and found, on my entrance, to my astonishment and delight, such a specimen (if all signs do not deceive me) of the work of the Holy Spirit as I have I think never before witnessed on a sick-bed, except in the case of _____, Rothesay." He catechized the boy, who answered with obvious understanding and love for the Savior. On May 2 he visited Wallace again "and found him rejoicing and advancing in knowledge as well as experience. He said he was ten days nearer death than when

---

9. McMullen, *God's Polished Arrow*, 31; Islay Burns, *Memoir*, 64.

10. William Burns to McCheyne, November 18, 1839, in Islay Burns, *Memoir*, 558–59.

11. Islay Burns, *Memoir*, 559.

12. McMullen, *God's Polished Arrow*, 145.

I last saw him, and this with joy. I asked him if he was not sorry. A. No; to me to live is Christ and to die is gain."[13] Tract distribution with others occupied part of his time.[14] He also spent time interviewing and praying with young communicants.[15]

Burns was prepared to listen to advice from ordinary members or adherents who had sat under McCheyne's ministry:

> May 21st—met with K.B____, the woman who sits in the pulpit stair. She said all head learning could not enable a man to feed the lambs; there must be first repentance, as in the case of Peter. She exhorted me with spiritual earnestness to watch for individual souls, saying, "You may lose a jewel from your crown; though you do not lose your crown, you may lose a jewel from it." She appeared to recognize the work of God in my soul, and spoke with great pleasure of the discourses of that day.[16]

He took the words to heart, because he was conscious of a "hungering after applause from man," which he sought to mortify.[17] All the time he labored he was praying for God to lay bare His arm in revival blessing.[18]

Burns continued on with the normal Sabbath services. St. Peter's had been full before; now it could not contain all who sought

---

13. Islay Burns, *Memoir*, 67–69, 74. On April 19, William Burns recorded, "Visited two poor sick people—no decided indication of spiritual life." Islay Burns, *Memoir*, 69.

14. Islay Burns, *Memoir*, 74.

15. Islay Burns, *Memoir*, 66–67, 70. On April 17, "Met with two young communicants.... They both appear hopeful converts to the Lord Jesus." On April 20, "Met with communicants again. Gave P. B. a token, and sent R. N. home to his closet, to meet me at a quarter past ten tomorrow, and see if he then wants a token."

16. Islay Burns, *Memoir*, 76.

17. Islay Burns, *Memoir*, 72. On June 21 he wrote in his journal, "I am vile, vile, vile, and feel myself most so when thanked for serving him." Islay Burns, *Memoir*, 78.

18. Islay Burns, *Memoir*, 72. "But O for a revival of that experimental deep-laid religion which Fleming valued and exemplifies so fully in his pages! 'Awake, awake, O arm of the Lord! Awake as in the ancient days, in the generations of old.' O for a spirit of humble wrestling prayer for the outpouring of the Holy Spirit that sinners may be awakened, and saints greatly edified and advanced."

admission. He continued also with the Thursday prayer meeting and the male and female classes, in all of which the attendance kept up. He later wrote to McCheyne that he found "not a few who seemed to have passed from death to life under your ministry."[19]

## A Defect in Burns's Preaching Rectified

In the early days of his time at St. Peter's, however, being concerned to make full proof of his ministry, Burns became aware of a deficiency in his application of certain gospel truths to his hearers. In particular he had been less than forthright regarding the state of fallen man and of the necessity of an unreserved surrender to the Lord Jesus Christ as prophet, priest, and king. Once this was rectified, his preaching went from strength to strength.[20] It was not long before one of the elders of St. Peter's could describe the impact of his preaching in these words:

> Scarcely had Mr. Burns entered on his work in St. Peter's here, when his power as a preacher began to be felt. Gifted with a solid and vigorous understanding, possessed of a voice of vast compass and power—unsurpassed even by that of Mr. Spurgeon—and withal fired with an ardour so intense and an energy so exhaustless that nothing could damp or resist it, Mr. Burns wielded an influence over the masses whom he addressed which was almost without parallel since the days of Wesley and Whitefield. Crowds flocked to St. Peter's from all the country round; and the strength of the preacher seemed to grow with the incessant demands made upon it.[21]

After several weeks people began approaching him to indicate the spiritual blessing they were receiving under his ministry. When one

---

19. Smellie, *Robert Murray McCheyne*, 104.

20. Islay Burns, *Memoir*, 88; McMullen, *God's Polished Arrow*, 32.

21. Islay Burns, *Memoir,* 61–62. Reverend Moody Stuart referred to Burns having "the irrepressible urgency of one standing between the living and the dead, the earnest pressing of salvation that would accept no refusal; himself standing consciously and evidently in the presence of the great God, with heaven and hell and the souls of men open before him, with Jesus Christ filling his heart with his love, and pouring grace into his lips, and with multitudes before him weeping for sorrow over discovered sin, or for joy in a discovered Savior." Islay Burns, *Memoir*, 63–64.

individual was awakened under a sermon on Psalm 71:16, he recorded in his journal: "O marvellous grace, that the Lord should regard at all my carnal, self-seeking ministry; to him be the glory *eternally.*"[22]

At the end of June he began a series of addresses on Colossians. On Sabbath afternoons he started to expound Psalm 130. He recorded some favorable symptoms of the presence of God in the congregation: two prayer meetings begun among the younger women and larger and livelier prayer meetings among the older members.[23] In his last three Sabbaths before going to Kilsyth, Burns was led "in a great measure to preach without writing." He did so that he might "study and pray for a longer time." The result of this was twofold: he felt more greatly helped by divine support, and the people were "more deeply solemnized," many being reduced to tears.[24] In the weeks to come he would benefit from adopting this approach, when there were so many meetings taking place during the week.

There was as yet one vital matter lacking—that his preaching would come with power. In this respect, both Islay Burns and Moody Stuart noted a discernible change in him after he went to Kilsyth. Before that date he was already "full of prayer; he seemed to care for nothing but to pray." As yet, however, the power that rested upon him did not affect his preaching, which was "sensible, clear, orthodox, unobjectionable." He had been "asking, seeking, knocking for the Holy Spirit; that Spirit came upon him with power, and the Lord added unto the church daily such as should be saved."[25]

## Revival Comes to Kilsyth, Then to Dundee
On July 16 Burns went to Kilsyth to assist at the Communion season in his father's church. Together with Alexander Somerville, he was used of God in a revival that is usually dated from July 23. Bonar recorded that "the Holy Spirit seemed to come down as a rushing mighty wind, and to fill the place. Very many were that day struck

---

22. Islay Burns, *Memoir*, 77.
23. Islay Burns, *Memoir*, 82.
24. Islay Burns, *Memoir*, 88.
25. Islay Burns, *Memoir*, 98–99.

to the heart; the sanctuary was filled with distressed and enquiring souls. All Scotland heard the glad news.... The Spirit in mighty power began to work from that day forward in many places of the land."[26]

Burns remained in Kilsyth for three weeks, assisting in the revival services and counseling inquirers. During this time a Mr. Lyon, missionary at Banton in the parish of Kilsyth, supplied for him at St. Peter's.[27] Burns returned to Dundee on Wednesday, August 8, hoping first to take some respite after his labors in Kilsyth. This was not to be, for he found himself almost immediately in the midst of a scene similar to that which he had just left. On the following day, at the end of the usual prayer meeting, Burns explained the reason for his delay. Many had, in any case, heard something of the movement at Kilsyth. He then invited those who felt the need of an outpouring of the Holy Spirit to convert them to remain behind. About one hundred did so. Burns addressed them, at the end of which "suddenly the power of God seemed to descend, and all were bathed in tears." The following night, as the congregation pressed into St. Peter's, "there was much melting of heart and intense desire after the Beloved of the Father." When the vestry door was opened for inquirers, a great number poured in with awful eagerness: "It was like a pent-up flood breaking forth; tears were streaming from the eyes of many, and some fell on the ground, groaning, and weeping, and crying for mercy."[28]

From that time on there were meetings held every day for many weeks, as various parts of the town were caught up in the awakening. Bonar summed up the proceedings by saying, "Many believers doubted; the ungodly raged; but the Word of God grew mightily and prevailed."[29] It was a work that no one man could cope with. Burns was ably assisted by evangelical ministers in the town: Baxter of Hill-

---

26. Andrew A. Bonar, *Memoir*, 109. See also Gillies, *Historical Collections of Accounts of Revival*, 556–58, being William Burns's account of the awakening at Kilsyth; Smellie, *Robert Murray McCheyne*, 106–7; Van Valen, *Constrained by His Love*, 308; and Islay Burns, *Memoir*, 98–96.

27. Islay Burns, *Memoir*, 560.

28. Andrew A. Bonar, *Memoir*, 114; Islay Burns, *Memoir*, 109.

29. Andrew A. Bonar, *Memoir*, 114; Islay Burns, *Memoir*, 109.

town Parish, Roxburgh of St. John's Parish, and Lewis of St. David's Parish. Neighboring ministers, like James Hamilton of Abernyte, were also deeply committed to the revival work. Some, like Horatius Bonar of Kelso, came a considerable distance to assist in the work. Other ministers, both from the town and farther afield, were happy to form part of the congregation and rejoice in the proceedings.[30]

Hamilton of Abernyte, part of the McCheyne circle of close friends, wrote to a colleague, Reverend J. Willis, toward the end of August:

> My dear Sir... You will have heard of the movement in St. Peter's, Dundee. I hope that much real good is going on. I have addressed Burns' congregation twice, on a week evening, and never met a more attentive or more impressed audience. He has had a meeting every night since Thursday fortnight, and so eager are the people to hear the Word, that every night he has an overflowing congregation. On the first three evenings there was much excitement among the people, and many (as at Kilsyth) cried out under the force of strong convictions. These expressions of feeling, and the lateness of the first meetings, have supplied a handle to gainsayers; but the work makes progress in spite of them, and from what I have seen and heard from Mr Burns, I have no doubt that there is a remarkable pouring out of the Spirit of God upon many.[31]

In his preoccupation with the various meetings, Burns had stopped keeping his journal. He resumed it again on August 24, two weeks into the revival time. He noted a crowded St. Peter's every night, "and many have been forced to go away without getting in." As well as preaching to the congregation, parts of the narrative of the revival under James Robe at Kilsyth a century earlier would be read to the people. At the end of August, Burns spoke to a packed congregation: "And in the afternoon every corner was filled, so that I could

30. Islay Burns, *Memoir*, 109–10.
31. William Arnot, *Life of James Hamilton*, 2nd ed. (London: James Nisbet, 1870), 143.

not, without much difficulty, force my way to the pulpit; hundreds were forced to be excluded."[32]

And so the work went on. There were meetings every night, with throngs of people waiting on the preaching. When not preaching, Burns and other ministers were occupied counseling inquirers, sometimes twenty, thirty, or fifty a day, the anxious praying alone or in groups while they waited to be spoken to personally. After the main services, many would remain behind for further instruction. Even after dismissal, many would attach themselves to the preacher as he retired to the vestry, in the hope of further counsel and prayer. Burns recorded for September 19: "When we left the session-house we met a great multitude still waiting to hear the Word, and some of them in tears. Many of these came along with Mr W____ and me to the west end of the town, and when we came to Roseangle, Mr W____ at my suggestion engaged with them in a parting prayer on the highway side, under the starlight faintly shining through the dark windy clouds."[33]

Open air preaching was not a feature of normal Presbyterian church life in Dundee. Burns made two attempts at this time. The first was to have been in the Meadows. The magistrates forbid this, so Burns, together with Reverend Baxter and Reverend Miller (assistant at St. David's and soon to be minister of Wallacetown), resorted instead to St. Peter's churchyard and held services for a large company. Burns commented: "I think the Spirit of God was much among the people of God on this occasion, filling them with joy and wonder at the free and infinite love of Jehovah." The second open air preaching was a week later in McKenzie Square.[34]

---

32. Islay Burns, *Memoir*, 110–11.

33. Islay Burns, *Memoir*, 119–20.

34. Islay Burns, *Memoir*, 111–12. Reverend John Bowes of the Christian Mission Church, who had often preached in the open air, in the Greenmarket, and in the Meadows fell foul of the magistrates and was eventually committed to trial for "wilful obstruction to the public thoroughfare" in June 1840. *The Autobiography or History of the Life of John Bowles* (Glasgow: G. Gallie & Son; Dundee: McGregor and Wise, 1872), 243–52; *Dundee, Perth, and Cupar Advertiser*, Friday, August 30, 1839; and the *Dundee Chronicle*, Thursday, June 25, 1840.

At this time, Burns's preaching was noted for its great fullness, its freedom, and its rich scriptural content as he expounded the Word and applied it with a melting and persuasive unction. In spite of the demands on him every night, there was a decided "clearness and force of thought and diction."[35] The man was very much in the message, and, like Bunyan, could have said, "I preached what I felt, what I smartingly did feel, even that under which my poor soul did groan and tremble to astonishment."[36] James Hamilton said of Burns that he was more distinguished by zeal for the glory of Christ than many who are more concerned for the salvation of sinners: "I do not say that he wants the other motives to ministerial fidelity, but I do say that every other is with him subordinated to that noblest of all, the *exaltation of Christ* in the salvation of souls."[37]

## A Typical Sabbath Day's Preaching

Burns records for October 6 a typical Sabbath day during the revival in his usual self-critical way:

> I rose at a quarter past nine, and felt very strong even after the incessant duties of Saturday.... In the forenoon I preached with much comfort, though not with much depth of experience or presence of the truth, from Romans iii, 20, 21. In the afternoon I preached from 1 John I, 3, last clause, and was much assisted than in the forenoon.... The congregation seemed much solemnized; I saw some young converts rejoicing greatly, and during the last Psalm a young woman was so deeply wounded that she could not restrain her feelings, and cried aloud for mercy from the Lord. In the evening I preached in Hilltown Church from Job xxxiii, 23, 24.... I was enabled to speak with some degree of tenderness both in expounding the truth and in afterwards applying it to men's hearts.... The

---

35. Islay Burns, *Memoir*, 121–22.

36. John Bunyan, *Grace Abounding to the Chief of Sinners*, in *The Works of John Bunyan*, ed. George Offor (Edinburgh: Banner of Truth Trust, 2009), 1:42.

37. Arnot, *Life of James Hamilton*, 143.

crowd was most dense, and many hundreds were standing without or obliged to go away. A blessed Sabbath.[38]

## A Testimony Recorded at the Time

William Middleton, a local printer, kept the public well informed of church affairs in the Dundee area. For example, in 1841 he printed the lectures on the physical, educational, and moral statistics of Dundee that George Lewis had delivered in December 1840. Prior to this he printed a small booklet that was the testimony of a young woman converted in the early weeks of the revival. Her case would be typical of many in those days, and of many of the working class who, in particular, were awakened and converted at that time. In her own words she described how she went from being wholly preoccupied with worldly pursuits to agreeing to go to hear the "word of man," and then becoming soundly converted and having a burden to witness to her unsaved friends. Her brother had commended Burns to her as a good minister, and "though he was young in years, he was far advanced in the divine life." Eventually she agreed to go, which she did for two months, but only to hear the "word of man." She described her heart as being as hard as adamant. She went back to St. Peter's when Burns got back from Kilsyth. One Sabbath morning he was preaching on Job 33:24: "Then he is gracious unto him, and saith, Deliver him from going down to the pit: I have found a ransom." Her testimony described how she came under conviction:

> About 11 pm that night the words that Mr B＿＿ was saying cut me to the heart. They were, "Young men and young women, oh! how long will you chase one another down to the pit? Will you still reject Christ, and him in the midst of you?"... My convictions grew deeper and deeper every day, until one night that I thought I saw the wrath of God coming down upon Christ for sin. Dear friends, I never felt the weight of sin before this; and then for two months, until I got a sight of Christ as a Savior, I felt as if on the very brink of hell. I saw

---

38. Islay Burns, *Memoir*, 122–23.

hell open for me, and the wrath of God ready to be poured out upon me!

Once she was sure of her salvation, she went on to witness to her unconverted friends of Christ freely offered in the gospel: "Dear friends, if you go away tonight without taking Christ perhaps you may open your eyes in hell tomorrow!"[39]

The revival may be said to have reached its climax at the October Communion. On that Sabbath evening there were three congregations—one in the church building and two others in adjoining school rooms. Burns commented, "During the whole of this communion Sabbath there was, I am told by the ministers, an unusually deep solemnity pervading the audience—the result, I trust, of the near presence of Jehovah."[40] For a time it was found necessary to hold the services in St. David's Church, it being the largest place of worship in Dundee, seating over two thousand people. The minister, Reverend George Lewis, himself heavily involved in the revival work at this time, welcomed this.

## The Testimony of Visiting Ministers

As news of the awakening spread, Dundee was visited by several men who came to assess the events for themselves. One such was Mr. Morgan of Belfast, who had heard of the extraordinary movement while in Ireland. Being in Scotland, he made his way to Dundee. There he met with Burns and two other ministers in early September. They conversed of the work in Kilsyth and Dundee. Morgan not only approved of the work but also agreed to preach for them, which he did from Romans 5:20–21.[41] Just a week later, while preaching at McKenzie Square, Burns found that he had in his audience Robert Haldane of Edinburgh and Caesar Malan of Geneva. Malan, in particular, was

---

39. *The Conversion of a Young Woman at St. Peter's, Dundee, in August 1839. Related by herself*, 3rd ed. (Dundee: William Middleton, 1841), 5–8.

40. Islay Burns, *Memoir*, 120–21.

41. Islay Burns, *Memoir*, 114 (September 4, 1839).

happy to preach in St. Peter's, which he did from John 14:27, and to be identified with the revival.[42]

In September also, Dr. John MacDonald of Ferintosh visited Dundee and preached for a week. It was during his time there that St. David's became the main meeting place, especially for evening services. He recorded in his journal how he preached for Burns in St. Peter's on the evening of his arrival (September 16) from Deuteronomy 32:39: "The house crowded; and the audience exhibited a solemnity and fixedness of attention rarely to be seen, and which evidently indicated an impression from above." MacDonald saw "tears in abundance" and "much silent weeping." He felt great liberty while preaching and a real sense of the presence of God. This was no doubt due in great measure to the thirty-nine prayer meetings, five of them led by children, which had been started in 1839 and which McCheyne was to learn of on his return (see chapter 5).

The following day MacDonald counseled sixteen people about the state of their souls, some of whom "obtained comfort." He recorded in his diary: "The work is evidently a work of God." Even when they moved to St. David's, with a much larger audience, there was the same solemnity and deep concern as before. MacDonald continued on for another week while Burns assisted at the Kilsyth Communion. He preached in the morning in St. Peter's and in the evening in St. David's. When not preaching, he spent his time counseling seekers and those under soul distress. Some of these were quite young. He spoke to two girls aged nine and a boy of eleven.[43]

One of the neighboring ministers, Alexander Cumming of Dunbarney Parish, Bridge of Earn, was invited by Burns to spend a week in Dundee in November in order to help out with the progress of the revival there. He preached every evening of that week. He kept a

---

42. Islay Burns, *Memoir*, 116–17. Malan did not believe as both McCheyne and Burns did, that assurance was of the essence of faith. Andrew A. Bonar, *Memoir*, 76–77.

43. John Kennedy, *The Apostle of the North: The Life and Labors of the Rev. John MacDonald, DD of Ferintosh* (Glasgow: Free Presbyterian Publications, 1978), 145–47.

record of his time there, commenting on what he observed in 1839 and also into 1840. He began by noting that those on whom a "supernatural change was wrought" belonged to every locality of the town, and not just St. Peter's Parish, "as if it were intended they should be salt impregnating the sinful mass of that manufacturing town, and neutralising the tendencies to moral corruption in every part of it."[44]

During the week he was in Dundee, Cumming was in St. Peter's daily. When not preaching, he was present at the meetings held for conference and prayer. He felt, like MacDonald and others, a real sense of the Lord's presence "in the awe with which the listening multitudes were penetrated, in the patience with which they heard the Word, and the prayerful ardour with which they followed up the exhortations of the pulpit."[45]

Cumming described how mill workers would pour out of the mills to attend services that had begun at 7:00 p.m., while they were still at work. They would be able to attend from around 8:00. A good number of those arriving late were men. These meetings would continue till 11:00 p.m. or later. Many remained behind under conviction of sin. On the Monday of the week Cumming was at St. Peter's, thirty young men between ages twenty and thirty were counseled in the session house: "Each of the thirty persons expressed pungent convictions, and then prayer, singing of Psalms and the exhibition of the terrors and mercies of the Lord followed till a little after eleven o'clock, when, as appeared afterwards, some really found Christ, and the rest had their impressions much deepened."[46]

It was not only at the services, during which there was a real sense of the need that "they must be saved then, or never," but also in the meetings organized after the main services were over that many found peace in believing in Jesus.[47]

---

44. Alexander Cumming, "Some Incidents Connected with the Revival in Dundee during the years 1839 and 1840," in Smellie, *Robert Murray McCheyne*, 234.

45. Smellie, *Robert Murray McCheyne*, 235.

46. Smellie, *Robert Murray McCheyne*, 235–36.

47. Smellie, *Robert Murray McCheyne*, 239–40.

During these revival weeks many boys, some as young as thirteen, who had stationed themselves on the pulpit stairs, listened "with the most riveted attention." On questioning them as to the length of time they had been seeking salvation (two months, three months, four months), Cumming pointed out God had been seeking them all their lives. On that occasion many were led to put their trust in the Savior. He noted how "not a few underwent a saving change. Some of them are now uttering Hosannahs in glory, while others, shot up to manhood, are fighting the battles of the Savior in this world below."[48]

Visiting and neighboring preachers found St. Peter's a good place to preach in, bathed as it was in so much prayer. Hamilton of Abernyte expressed the view of many: "It was pleasant to preach in St. Peter's Church. The children on the pulpit stairs, the prayers in the vestry, the solemn and often crowded auditory, the sincerity of all the worship, and the often-felt presence of God, made it like few other sanctuaries. It was only on week-evenings that I was ever there, but perhaps they were more remarkable than even the Sabbaths."[49]

### Conclusion of Burns's Short Pastorate

Burns's temporary pastorate at St. Peter's came to an end in November. In his self-effacing way, he attributed the revival blessing in large part to the prayers of their absent pastor, who had been praying for them even on his sickbed in Smyrna[50] when revival came: "But most of all do I believe that your prayers for your people have been answered in this work of the Lord. Indeed, I do not know how far dependent it may be all found to be on your wrestlings in the Holy Spirit in behalf of your flock, both while among them, and while absent on the Lord's chosen errand."[51]

On the Sabbath of November 17, Burns gave his farewell sermon as pastor, though he would preach occasionally later. He addressed them on John 15, union to Christ. He recorded in his journal, "The

---

48. Smellie, *Robert Murray McCheyne*, 236–37.
49. Arnot, *Life of James Hamilton*, 152–53.
50. Bonar, *Memoir*, 108–9; Van Valen, *Constrained by His Love*, 299.
51. Islay Burns, *Memoir*, 561.

season was indeed one that I shall never forget. Before me there was a crowd of immortal souls all hastening to eternity, some to heaven, and many I fear to hell, and I was called to speak to them, as it were, for the last time, to press Jesus on them, and to beseech them to be reconciled to God by the death of his Son."[52]

After the sermon, Burns intimated McCheyne would be back with them on Thursday. The parting that evening showed the deep affection the people of St. Peter's had for him.[53] Thus ended what Yeaworth has called phase 1 of the revival—spontaneous movements within the parishes of Kilsyth and Dundee, "where the local ministers had prepared the way for Burns and were as instrumental in the actual awakening. Here the revival was essentially within the parishes."[54]

---

52. Islay Burns, *Memoir*, 128.

53. Islay Burns, *Memoir*, 129:

> The people retired very slowly when we had dismissed about five o'clock, and many waited in the passage and in the gallery until I retired, who wept much when I was passing along, and obliged me to pray with them in the passage again. When I came out I met with many of the same affecting tokens of the reality of my approaching separation from a people among whom the Lord, in His sovereign and infinite mercy, has shown me the most marvellous proofs of his covenant love, and from among whom, I trust, he has taken, during my continuance among them, not a few jewels to shine in the crown of Emmanuel the Redeemer! Glory to the Lamb that was slain.

54. Yeaworth, "Robert Murray McCheyne," 298.

# 5

# McCheyne's Last Years in Dundee: Continuing Evidence of Revival

I preached same evening [as he arrived]. I never saw such an assembly in a Church before…. There was not a spot in the church left unoccupied. Every passage and stair were filled. I was almost overpowered by the sight, but felt great liberty in preaching from 1 Cor. II, 1–4. I never before preached to such an audience—so many weeping—so many waiting as for the words of Eternal Life. I never heard such sweet singing anywhere—so tender and affecting, as if the people felt they were praising a present God. When I came out of the Church the whole of the Church road was filled with the people old and young and I had to shake hands 10 at a time…. There is evidently a great change upon the people here. And tho' it is to be expected that many are mere naturally awakened and excited yet I see a great many who I feel confident are savingly changed. On Sabbath I heard Burns in the morning and evening and I preached in the afternoon—It was a very solemn day—2 Chron. V, 13–14 was my text and Burns preached on "the throne of grace" Heb. IV. He is certainly a very remarkable preacher. The plainness and force of his statements and his urgency I never saw equalled. He has a very clear view of divine things and an amazing power of voice and body. But above all God seems really to accompany his preaching with demonstration of the Spirit. I find him in private much more humble and single hearted than I could have believed from the reports circulated…. I have no desire but the salvation of my people by whatever instrument. I have found out many souls saved under my own ministry that I did not know of

before. They are not afraid to come out now. It has become so
common a thing to be concerned about the soul.... My body
is much stronger than when I was with you. As long as I have
Burns with me I shall work but partly. My people pray for my
complete recovery and I believe that through their prayer I
may be quite restored.

—Robert Murray McCheyne to his parents,
November 26, 1839

In a letter to Candlish written from London, McCheyne related how
he and Bonar first heard in Hamburg, after five months of silence, of
how "God had visited our beloved Church in a remarkable manner."
They now felt "like men that dream." McCheyne immediately linked
this good news with their endeavors to seek the blessing and salvation of Israel.[1] There was, however, a timely and tactful letter from
Candlish waiting for McCheyne in London. Candlish sensed something of the delicacy of the situation of McCheyne returning to
resume his duties where another had been so greatly used of God:

We hear much that is cheering and encouraging of what is
going on at Dundee. At the same time, there are circumstances
which lead me to suggest, that it will be very necessary for you,
coming in at this particular stage of the work, to proceed with
due caution and deliberation, and even in some particulars
with a certain reserve and suspense of judgment for a time. I
say this to you frankly and confidentially. And I think it right
to take the earliest opportunity of saying it: being very sure
that you will not misunderstand me.... I can not conceal from

---

1. *Familiar Letters by the Rev. Robert Murray McCheyne, edited by his father*
(Edinburgh: John Johnstone, 1848), 171–72. As he sailed up the Thames, McCheyne
wrote to his parents: "We have heard something of a reviving work at Kilsyth—we
saw it noticed in one of the newspapers. I also saw the name of Dundee associated
with it, so that I earnestly hope good has been doing in our church and the dew from
on high watering our parishes, and that the flocks whose pastors have been wandering may also share in the blessing. We are quite ignorant of the facts, and you may
believe are very anxious to hear." Andrew A. Bonar, *Memoir*, 113 (November 6, 1839).

you that there are, so far as I have heard, some things likely to occasion some little difficulty and some points of considerable delicacy. And I feel persuaded that both in regard to the wholesome progress of the work at Dundee, and the general cause of the revival of religion, and the judgment to be formed respecting it, much may depend upon you. But I speak very much from report and I entreat you not to suppose that I am at all disposed to view with a cold eye what is going on.... Meantime let us earnestly pray that we may not be backward in such a matter as this and yet that we may have wisdom. Excuse these loose and hasty hints.[2]

Candlish's words were far from explicit. One obvious difficulty to overcome was the transition that would take place as McCheyne once again resumed his pastorate. How would he respond to the fact that the inexperienced Burns was the vessel used of God in the awakening in his absence? There is no doubt that both McCheyne and Burns had endeared themselves to the congregation attending St. Peter's. Some in the congregation, however, who had listened to Burns nightly for weeks not only thought highly of him but also saw him as a more powerful preacher than McCheyne, perhaps hoping he could continue on at St. Peter's.[3]

As matters worked out, Candlish's fears were allayed for several reasons. First, the spirit that both McCheyne and Burns showed displayed a complete absence of rivalry—rather, a rejoicing in the way God had chosen to work. Burns recorded in his journal:

Had a letter from dear Mr McCheyne, written in a spirit of joy for the work of the Lord, which shows a great triumph, I think, of divine grace over the natural jealousy of the human heart. O Lord, I would praise thee with all my heart for this, and would entreat that when thy dear servant the pastor of this people is restored to them, he may be honoured a

---

2. R. S. Candlish to McCheyne, November 8, 1839, MACCH 2.1.80.

3. Arnot, *Life of James Hamilton*, 141; John S. Ross, *Time for Favour: Scottish Mission to the Jews 1838–1852* (Stoke-on-Trent, England: Tentmaker Publications, [2011]), 164–65, as quoted in Lennie, *Land of Many Revivals*, 332n64.

hundredfold more in winning souls to Christ than I have been in thine infinite and sovereign mercy. Amen.[4]

As to McCheyne, his traveling companion Bonar recorded how he responded to the news of the awakening in Dundee: "They were such as made his heart rejoice. He had no envy at another instrument having been so honoured in the place where he himself had laboured with many tears and temptations. In true Christian magnanimity, he rejoiced that the work of the Lord was done, by whatever hand. Full of praise and wonder, he set his foot once more on the shore of Dundee."[5]

A second reason for concern was the possibility that recent converts from the revival months might "regard their spiritual father in a light in which they could regard none besides." McCheyne, however, exhibited a "holy disinterestedness that suppressed every feeling of envy." All that mattered to him was "the salvation of my people, by whatever instrument."[6]

A third problem that could have arisen was what Burns should do now that McCheyne had returned. They met together in McCheyne's manse on the evening of November 23. They proceeded to the Thursday prayer meeting, prayed together, and then both preached. Burns recorded in his journal that he found McCheyne to be in "but weak health," and prayed that he might be restored to full strength and become "the means of winning many souls for Jesus."[7] For his part, McCheyne wrote to Burns, thanking him for all his labors in Dundee and for how he had been an answer to prayer. By the end of December, when Burns was about to be part of another time of awakening in Perth along with the recently appointed Reverend John Milne of St. Leonards, McCheyne wrote to him. He would have liked him to stay in Dundee: "You know I told you my mind plainly, that I thought the Lord had so blessed you in Dundee, that you were called to a fuller

---

4. Islay Burns, *Memoir*, 128.
5. Andrew A. Bonar, *Memoir*, 115.
6. Andrew A. Bonar, *Memoir*, 116.
7. Islay Burns, *Memoir*, 130.

and deeper work there; but if the Lord accompanies you to other places, I have nothing to object."[8] The Lord was indeed to accompany Burns, as he first spent several months in Perth, though he intended initially to stay only one night.[9] Wherever he went thereafter blessing followed, as phase 2 of the revival got under way.

## Burns's Second Time in Dundee

Correspondence continued between McCheyne and Burns, the latter returning to preach in Dundee from time to time, especially from December 5, 1840, to April 1, 1841, in Dudhope Parish Church.[10] During these months he not only preached for McCheyne during his illness in March but also undertook a punishing schedule of meetings in Dudhope Church, the Gaelic church, and several schools: "The meetings in these schools were of deepest interest. Many were

---

8. Andrew A. Bonar, *Memoir*, 119–20.

9. Burns wrote to McCheyne that he had decided to remain in Perth to assist Reverend Milne instead of returning to St. Peter's for January 1: "Dense crowds come out from night to night to our meetings in St. Leonard's Church: and many come in the forenoons to converse privately about their state, some of them seeming to be deeply convinced of sin, and others who seem to be the children of God being evidently refreshed and quickened in their devotedness to the Lord Jesus. A great many prayer meetings are in the course of being formed, the work of the Lord continues to deepen here." MACCH 2.4.6.

The Rev. Milne wrote to a colleague, Mr. Edmond:

> I have been busy, very busy, almost unceasingly, night and day, for the last six weeks; and the result of the labor, I trust, one of the most hopeful and widest revivals that has as yet taken place in Scotland. The person chiefly instrumental in beginning and carrying on this is Mr Burns, lately of Dundee, who is living with me; and we are very happy, working without intermission.... You can form no idea of what a thirst there is on the part of the people to hear; and we have already much fruit in numerous cases of hopeful conversion. I have every day fresh reason to bless God that I was sent here.

Horatius Bonar, *Life of the Rev. John Milne of Perth*, 4th ed. (London: James Nisbet, 1868), 20–21 (February 10, 1840).

10. Islay Burns, *Memoir*, 141–58; McMullen, *God's Polished Arrow*, 47–78 (chap. 3); Lennie, *Land of Many Revivals*, 335, 338–53, 356–60, 387–89, 394–99; W. J. Couper et al., *Scotland Saw His Glory: A History of Revivals in Scotland*, ed. Richard Owen Roberts (Wheaton, Ill.: International Awakening Press, 1995), 279–88.

brought under conviction at them. These humble buildings were the scenes of poignant sorrow and jubilant joy, when not a few deeply exercised were brought to the Savior."[11]

Burns visited the soldiers in their barracks, handing out tracts and books and preaching to them on Thursdays at three o'clock. In addition, he spoke to the mill workers outside the various mills, visited the sick, and debated with Romanists, socialists, and sceptics. He encountered some opposition from "roughs," particularly the unemployed and poor, for some of whom he provided meals in his lodgings. Many from the mills or factories professed salvation during his time with them. Some people tried to get him to stay on as pastor, but he resisted this, convinced he was called to do the work of an itinerant evangelist, and took off for Edinburgh.[12]

## McCheyne's Assessment of the Impact of Revival

McCheyne was well placed to assess the impact of the revival. He was returning after a year's absence to a people he had labored among. His assessment was nothing if not realistic. In a letter to his sister, Eliza, toward the end of the year, he said, "There are a good many seeking souls just now.... There are also many that seem to have found Christ and esteem Him the pearl of great price. But the greatest change of all is among the Christians. They are so much happier, gentle and more loving than they used to be. Still the great mass are as I left them, or rather hardened by seeing the work on others."[13]

In a sermon on Hebrews 2:10 ("bringing many sons unto glory"), he said that after all the awakening there had been, "few have found the gate. Many were left unawakened, some sought but did not find. Few there be that find it."[14] There were many also who still persisted in thinking that coming to faith in Christ was some "strange act of the mind, different from believing what God has said of His Son."[15]

---

11. Inglis, *Notes of the History of Dudhope Free Church*, 12.
12. Inglis, *Notes of the History of Dudhope Free Church*, 12–14.
13. McCheyne to Eliza, December 31, 1839, MACCH 2.1.91.
14. McCheyne, *Passionate Preacher*, 247.
15. McCheyne to Bonar, December 2, 1839, in Andrew A. Bonar, *Memoir*, 118.

## The Revival Prayer Meetings Reported to McCheyne

One of the most gratifying aspects of the revival, McCheyne discovered, was how the whole had been bathed in prayer, showing something of the reality, depth, and power behind the work. When he left Dundee, there were four prayer meetings. On his return he found thirty-nine, five of those being for children. On request, some gave reports of their private meetings. Jane Petrie wrote to him on December 11 of a fellowship meeting, a prayer meeting basically (see chapter 7), which had been held on Sabbath morning for some time: "We had it before the work of God began, but it has been laid aside for this some time on account of so many mor (*sic*) meetings and Sermon being in the Church every evening." They had been meeting on Sabbath morning at 7 a.m. in the home of James Wallace of Paton's Lane. They read the Word without comment, sang psalms, and engaged in prayer. They had intended to start another one on Fridays, but revival came.[16]

Another report was by Alexander Laing, who was desperate to tell his pastor, first, that the Lord had "redeemed him from the lowest hell." Then he informed of how his father had allowed him to have a prayer meeting on Monday and on Saturday nights with his companions in the house, "to pray for God's blessing on themselves and others."[17] Laing and John Paton also conducted a meeting for the elderly on Sundays at 7 p.m. in the home of Louisa Lindsay of Tait's Lane in the Hawkhill area.[18]

David Kay described the one held in his house as a close meeting, consisting of praise, prayer, reading of the Word, and a consideration of a question from the Shorter Catechism or a passage of Scripture. They first met on Wednesdays at 8 p.m., and then reverted to Saturday mornings. There was also a Sabbath midday meeting. Kay concluded his report by writing, "Dear Sir, I have been professing to teach a Sabbath evening school for 20 years and more but never did

---

16. Jane Petrie to McCheyne, December 11, 1839, MACCH 2.1.86.
17. Alexander Laing to McCheyne, December 12, 1839, MACCH 2.5.6.
18. Robertson, *Awakening*, 171.

I all my life before have such a pleasant school as I have now. O how blessed and happy it is when Zion's Mighty King comes in the Power and Glory of His grace among a people."[19] Another prayer meeting that Kay supervised was for children, and it was held in the home of Mrs. Sime. It consisted of Sabbath scholars, the oldest being twelve or thirteen, taught by Kay. They had been told they were too young to pray, so they met in the open air in a secluded area. Then Thomas Sime, one of their teachers, allowed the use of his house. They met every Sabbath night after school until 9 p.m. "to pray for a blessing on the instructions we get at the school and in the church." The Word was read, they sang and prayed, "and then [went] to our home to our closet." They closed their letter by promising to pray for McCheyne "and for the dear servant of God that has laboured amongst us in your absence."[20]

Thomas Brown reported on a children's prayer meeting thirty strong, using a classroom granted by Mrs. Isles. None of them were older than fourteen years of age. They had persevered in spite of opposition and were keen for McCheyne to visit them. The letter was signed by Thomas Brown and John Smith, eighteen boys and twelve girls appending their signatures. They met every night at 6 o'clock and also on Sabbath mornings for singing praise to God, prayer, and reading Scripture.

From Agnes Crow and others, McCheyne received a letter that, for all its poor spelling and punctuation, breathed a profound gratitude both for the prayers of McCheyne and the labors of Burns. Burns had been a chosen vessel of God: "You often prayed for your church to become a Bochim a place of weeping and it has not failed to be in evening even when it was late when the Spirit of God came among us with power to break the rocky hearts in pieces and made the tears to steal down the cheek that never was seen to weep for sin before."[21]

---

19. David Kay to McCheyne, December 24, 1839, MACCH 2.5.8.
20. Thomas Sime and others to McCheyne, December 9, 1839, MACCH 2.5.2.
21. Agnes Crow and others to McCheyne, November 30, 1839, MACCH 2.5.1.

Mrs. Catherine Likely wrote to McCheyne, referring to "a precious season of refreshing from the presence of the Lord." She traced this to early July, when Burns preached for three Sabbaths on Psalm 130: "That was the first time that the Spirit was really felt by a number of the people of God." She detailed the meetings, then concluded by saying how many had been brought to Christ of whom Burns was not aware, "who really are shining lights," and a "great number under your own ministry whom none knew of till this present time."[22] All in all these prayer meetings were orderly, whether open or close, with very little exhortation being given. While McCheyne feared the high point of the Spirit's work had passed by, he trusted that it would return "in greater power than ever."[23]

## Evidence of Revival Work Continuing

McCheyne now had the daunting task of seeking to carry on the work that had flourished under Burns. The day after he returned to Dundee, November 24, 1839, he preached at St. Peter's from 2 Chronicles 5:13–14, the glory of the Lord filling the house, and he also referenced Pentecost:

> My dearly beloved flock, it is my heart's desire and prayer that this very day might be such a day among us—that God would indeed open the windows of heaven, as he has done in the past, and pour down a blessing, till there be no room to receive it. My dear flock, I am deeply persuaded there will be no full, soul-filling, heart nourishing, heart-satisfying out-pouring of the Spirit of God, till there be more praise and thanking the Lord.... The Lord gave you my dear brother to care for your souls; and far better than that—for to give you a man only would have been a poor gift—he has given you His Holy Spirit.[24]

---

22. Mrs. Likely to McCheyne, December 5, 1839, MACCH 2.5.3.

23. McCheyne to Andrew Bonar, December 2, 1839, in Bonar, *Memoir*, 118–19.

24. McCheyne, *From the Preacher's Heart*, 120–21. Bonar wrote of that first Thursday back that "many a face was seen anxiously gazing on their restored pastor;

There were many evidences, however, of the Spirit still at work in those who attended St. Peter's. His diary for December 8, 1839, records: "Saw J.T. in fever. She seems really in Christ now; tells me how deeply my words sank into her soul when I was away. A.M. stayed to tell me her joy. J.B. walked home with me, telling me what God had done for his soul, when one day I had stopt (*sic*) at the quarry on account of a shower of rain, and took shelter with my pony in the engine-house." McCheyne had pointed to the fire in the furnace, asking, "What does that remind you of?"—words that had gone home to his heart. Three days later he noted that a woman came to see him who had been away from church fellowship for twenty years but whom McCheyne had spoken to two years earlier (1837) when he followed up his visitation by preaching in a green on Ezekiel 20:43, "And there shall ye remember your ways, and all your doings, wherein ye have been defiled; and ye shall loathe yourselves in your own sight for all your evils that ye have committed." She came trembling to McCheyne, asking for restoration to fellowship.[25]

In March 1840, he recorded various responses to his preaching: one woman crying out bitterly, a young man coming to tell him that he had found Christ, yet another under conviction being persecuted by her father. He commented, "Roll on, thou river of life! Visit every dwelling! Save a multitude of souls. Come, Holy Spirit! Come quickly!"[26]

The following month he noted a congregation very much affected by the preaching, so that "the church was filled with sobbing. Many whom I did not know were now affected." That particular evening, April 20, the people were not dismissed until midnight: "Many followed us. One, in great agony, prayed she might find Christ that very night."[27]

---

many were weeping under the unhealed wounds of conviction." Andrew A. Bonar, *Memoir*, 115.

25. Andrew A. Bonar, *Memoir*, 123.
26. Andrew A. Bonar, *Memoir*, 126.
27. Andrew A. Bonar, *Memoir*, 128.

Further evidence of the Spirit at work is recorded after his first trip to Ireland in July 1840, when he spoke on Psalm 51:12–13, "Restore unto me the joy of thy salvation." There was much of the Spirit of God on that occasion: "First one crying out in extreme agony, then another. Many were deeply melted and all solemnised. Felt a good deal of freedom in speaking of the glory of Christ's salvation. Coming down, I spoke quietly to some whom I knew to be under deep concern. They were soon heard together weeping bitterly; many more joined them.... Their cries were often bitter and piercing, bitterest when the freeness of Christ was pressed upon them."[28]

## A Typical Convert of the Revival Days

Alexander Cumming of Dunbarney Parish, who had assisted Burns in November 1839 and thereafter Milne at Perth, was present to help McCheyne in 1840. He left his impressions of the progress of the gospel in that year, and in particular a good example of one whose seeking and finding of Christ over quite a period of time shows that many of those who professed faith in those days were not making empty professions or hasty decisions. A lady from Clunie, who had long been in a state of great distress about her soul, even to despair, made her way to Dundee early in 1840 to listen to the ministry of McCheyne and other ministers. She recalled her experience in a letter written twenty years later in 1860. She first heard McCheyne in Wallacetown Church one Sabbath evening, speaking on the need for the new birth. This was the beginning of an awakening for her, as she realized—"I felt that I had not undergone this change." She began to search the Scriptures. The next time she heard McCheyne, it was on Revelation 14:13, "Blessed are the dead which die in the Lord." She recalled vividly how he stood before his congregation, having "held up Christ freely to the unconverted present," then ended by saying Christ would be swift witness against them eternally. That evening she spoke with McCheyne: "He prayed with me, and told me he would remember me at the throne of grace." Cumming and

---

28. Andrew A. Bonar, *Memoir*, 134.

McCheyne then went up to Huntly to administer Communion. After that, when McCheyne went to Edinburgh for the convocation, Cumming supplied in his place. It was while he was preaching on Christ washing the disciples' feet that the lady in question entered into salvation: "Her long tossed vessel got into the haven, and from much conversation which I had with her at that period, and during the last ten years, and from her holy and consistent walk, I cannot doubt but that this was the time of love, when Jesus passed by and said unto her, 'Live!'"[29] Her narrative described the peace and joy she then experienced and the delight she had in reading her Bible. She was so happy she longed to depart and be with the Lord. Her narrative ends with these words: "May the Lord give me grace to be ever living in preparation for that great change, and sooner or later, I shall enter into the joy of my Lord, and sing that song of praise which shall never terminate through all eternity. Amen."[30] Cumming remarked that her case was typical of many who for some considerable time had been in great distress of soul. He found several he conversed with that weekend had a similar testimony.[31]

## A Further Time of Awakening

As late as 1842, there were still evidences of awakenings taking place, including one lady who was converted just months before her death. On May 22 of that year, McCheyne recorded in his diary:

> I have seen some very evident awakenings of late. J.G. awakened partly through the word preached, and partly through the faithful warnings of her fellow servant, A.R., who has been for about a year in the deepest distress, seeking rest, but finding none. R.M. converted last winter at the Tuesday meeting in Annefield. She was brought very rapidly to peace with God, and to a calm, sedate, prayerful state of mind.... She was to be admitted at last communion, but caught fever before the Sabbath. On Tuesday last, she died in great peace and joy. When

---

29. Smellie, *Robert Murray McCheyne*, 240–47.
30. Smellie, *Robert Murray McCheyne*, 248.
31. Smellie, *Robert Murray McCheyne*, 249.

she felt death coming on, she said, "O death, death, come! Let us sing." Many that knew her have been a good deal moved homeward by this solemn providence.[32]

It was not only people from the Dundee area who entered into the blessings of salvation. In a letter to a soul inquiring after Jesus, McCheyne made reference to a visit from a young woman whom he had not seen before. Having come from another part of Scotland, she attended St. Peter's, where she learned of her sinfulness and need of Christ. "About four weeks ago she found rest and joy at the Savior's feet. I said to her 'Then you will bless God that He brought you from your own country to this place.' She said 'I often do that.'"[33]

In the autumn of 1842, James B. Hay, assistant to Horatius Bonar in Kelso and heavily involved in the revival work there, paid a visit to Dundee. He wrote to a friend of "much to tell you of what the Lord has done and is doing in this town." In the house in which he was staying, there were three meetings a week being held, at which he often spoke: "And never did I witness such interesting scenes.... The number on Sabbath nights, within the last two months has increased from sixty to seventy to nearly two hundred. Most of them are mill girls, and many of them have truly become members of the family of God."[34]

McCheyne's diary has no entries after early 1843. One last case of awakening is recorded for January 6: "Heard of an awakened soul finding rest—true rest, I trust. Two new cases of awakening; both very deep and touching. At the very time when I was beginning to give up in despair, God gives me tokens of His presence returning."[35]

## McCheyne Still Not Content, in Spite of the Blessing

He wrote in his diary of despairing for two reasons. He believed that a faithful minister should expect to see fruit for his labors in the gospel. He was also never content with what had been accomplished and was

---

32. Andrew A. Bonar, *Memoir*, 142.

33. Andrew A. Bonar, *Memoir*, 319.

34. I. Walker, *Memoir of the Rev. James Ballantyne Hay* (Edinburgh, 1870), 16–18, as quoted in Lennie, *Land of Many Revivals*, 334–35.

35. Andrew A. Bonar, *Memoir*, 147–48; Van Valen, *Constrained by His Love*, 411.

still critical of the spiritual state of the town, even after it had been visited by revival. He unburdened himself in this latter regard in a lecture on Capernaum (Matt. 11:20–24):

> Scotland, in like manner, has been exalted to heaven. We have not had the personal presence of Christ, like Capernaum, but we have had the same message which he carried.... Dundee has been exalted to heaven.... You have had a thousand such days of mercy, yet how few of you have improved them!... We have had more of the Holy Spirit poured out than ever Capernaum had. I do not know that any country has been visited this way, as Scotland has been.[36]

He described St. Peter's as a congregation exalted to heaven, yet notwithstanding all the souls saved and "all the mighty works Jesus has done, multitudes have never come." Many had "wondered at Christ's mighty work" but had not left their sin: "The taverns are as many as ever, these dens of iniquity are not diminished; the number of brawlers on the Saturday night and Sabbath is not smaller. If Jesus were here He would upbraid you."[37] He concluded by referring to the clear teaching of the Bible on degrees of suffering in hell. Those who sinned against gospel light would receive the greater damnation.[38]

## Visitation Resumed

Faced with such a situation, McCheyne resumed his pastoral duties unrelentingly. He was determined to continue on with visitation and catechizing. He noted in his diary on April 7, 1840: "Impressed tonight with the complete necessity of preaching to my people in their own lanes and closes; in no other way will God's word ever reach them."[39] To do so would ground the people more deeply in divine things and enable him to get to grips with hypocrites and the unconverted. A few months later, however, he had to admit, in a let-

---

36. McCheyne, *From the Preacher's Heart*, 531 (full text, 529–35).
37. McCheyne, *From the Preacher's Heart*, 533.
38. McCheyne, *From the Preacher's Heart*, 534.
39. Andrew A. Bonar, *Memoir*, 126.

ter to Burns, that though he wanted, health permitting, "to catechise through [his] parish," he felt "the immense difficulty of it in a town, and such a neglected, ignorant one as this."[40] Bonar, who knew him well, noted that while he could cope with the preaching and teaching, the house-to-house visitation was really by this time beyond his physical capabilities.[41] Eventually Mr. Gatherer was appointed as assistant minister at St. Peter's in October 1842 to help in particular with essential visitation work.[42] To assist him in this four more elders were ordained, and a fifth admitted, "who will all, I trust, be a blessing in this place when I am gone," McCheyne wrote.[43]

What visitation McCheyne was able to do, and he got back into it quickly, gave clear evidence of God having been at work in the hearts of many. He noted for January 2, 1840, how he visited six families, where he spoke of the Word made flesh and was "refreshed and solemnised at each of them." He was then visited in the evening by some others. One was a "believing little boy." Another came to him complaining she could not come to Christ for the hardness of her heart. Yet another spoke of how she had once been awakened under his preaching, then gone back, but at the Communion had been brought to Christ under Horatius Bonar's ministry. She was standing firm in spite of persecution from both her parents.[44]

McCheyne also continued his use of deaconesses for visiting women. In a letter to a Miss Katherine Duncan, he asked, "Will you do me the favour to call for Elspeth Robertson any day of this week, the old woman you spoke of above the Lows in Tait's Lane—and tell me whether you think the Lord has opened her heart to believe in

---

40. Andrew A. Bonar, *Memoir*, 288–89.

41. Andrew A. Bonar, *Memoir*, 159.

42. Managers' Minutes of St. Peter's Church, April 7, 1841; December 10, 1842: "to look out for an assistant in his out door labors."

43. McCheyne to Mr. Alexander Smith, November 15, 1842, Dundee City Archives, MS CH3/338/58/1; McCheyne to Mr. Alexander Smith, January 28, 1843, Dundee City Archives, MS CH3/338/58/2.

44. Andrew A. Bonar, *Memoir*, 125.

Jesus. You can understand a woman's heart better than I can do."[45]
McCheyne continued until just before his death to be involved in
the distribution of tracts, some of which he wrote himself,[46] to every
house in the town.[47]

## Ministerial Prayer Meetings

Those of the Bonar and McCheyne circle set aside time on Saturday
evenings to pray for each other's engagements on the Lord's Day.[48]
They were concerned increasingly to see that a spirit of prayer was
continued in the town, notwithstanding the private prayer meetings
which had commenced during 1839. Soon after his return from Palestine, a ministerial prayer meeting was begun. This took place every
Monday at 11 a.m. and lasted an hour and a half. Writing to Burns,
who was now in Perth, McCheyne said, "This is a great comfort, and
may be a great blessing. Of course, we do not invite the colder ministers; that would only damp our meeting."[49] The evangelical ministers,
like Lewis of St. David's, Roxburgh of St. John's, Baxter of Hilltown
Church, and others, met first for a time of prayer together. They had
also selected beforehand a topic for discussion relative to their ministerial duties. McCheyne gained great benefit from these occasions,
and only essential duties kept him from attending. He recorded his
impressions of these mornings in his diary:

> 8 Dec. [1839] This has been a deeply interesting week. On
> Monday our ministerial prayer-meeting was set going in St.
> David's vestry. The hearts of all seem really in earnest in it.

---

45. McCheyne to Miss Katherine Duncan, January 14, 1840, Dundee City
Archives, MS TD 87/1.

46. For example, in his tract "What Does It Mean to Be Saved?," he emphasized
a sovereign God and the sovereignty of the Holy Spirit. Yet he urged even the awakened to cry night and day to God that He would reveal Christ unto them.

47. Andrew A. Bonar, *Memoir*, 325. McCheyne "to one who had lately taken
up the cross," January 31, 1843: "Tonight we have been at a large meeting about the
tracts which are distributed monthly to every house in town—a very sweet society."

48. Andrew A. Bonar, *Memoir*, 52.

49. McCheyne to Burns, December 2, 1839, in Andrew A. Bonar, *Memoir*,
129–30.

The Lord answers prayer; may it be a great blessing to our souls and to our flocks. 30 Dec. Pleasant meeting of ministers. Many delightful texts on "Arguments to be used with God in prayer." How little I have used these. Should we not study prayer more?[50]

A short while later Burns wrote to McCheyne to remind him of a proposal made while he was in Dundee of a day of solemn fasting and prayer. Perth was about to start one at St. Leonard's. He urged his friend to "try unitedly with solemn humiliation at the foot of the cross for all those sins which have hitherto obstructed the progress of the Lord's work, for an abundant outpouring of the Holy Ghost upon the Church and especially on these two cities with the adjacent country."[51]

## Applicants for Communion Interviewed Carefully

Coming back to a parish blessed by revival, McCheyne found his work cut out coping with those who wished to be communicant members of St. Peter's. Moreover, the fact that numbers were pressing for admission and had a serious interest in spiritual matters is evident from the desire for additional Communion services. McCheyne decided to dispense Communion once a quarter instead of the traditional once a year.[52] "The communions," wrote Robertson, "were an excellent way of ensuring that those who were converted were added to the church and its membership."[53] Before admission, however, McCheyne, as before, conducted his communicant classes prior to Communion dates, interviewing each individual. The extant notebooks detailing his interviews (October 1840 to October 1842) show how he built upon information provided by Burns in his absence. Some of those interviewed he classed as "ignorant," "anxious," "sincere," or "in earnest." One fourteen-year-old, Margaret Yule, he recorded as "anxious to come under Mr Burns, seems really a child

50. Andrew A. Bonar, *Memoir*, 130.
51. Burns to McCheyne, February 26, 1840, MACCH 2.4.9.
52. Andrew A. Bonar, *Memoir*, 129.
53. Robertson, *Awakening*, 169.

of God tho' it is hard to know." He looked for clear signs of spiritual life. One applicant, eighteen-year-old Jean Crawford of Mid Wynd, had approached McCheyne in October 1840 but was not admitted. The following March, he could record: "Has found Christ since last time. Not very bright, but I think sincere." He would always err on the side of admission. Of fourteen-year-old Isobel Bain of Perth Road he wrote: "Still cares for her soul, and loves Jesus. The blood of Christ gives me peace. Christ is precious to me. Answers well. Admitted." Of sixteen-year-old David Dewar he wrote: "For two years thinks he has found Christ. Sweet lad. Admitted." Twenty-four applicants out of thirty-six were admitted to the April 1842 Communion.[54]

One of the features of the revival was the number of young people awakened or converted. Even prior to the January 1840 Communion, two youngsters under eleven, four aged fourteen, and three who were fifteen or sixteen had applied to be admitted.[55] Age, however, was not a barrier to McCheyne. When challenged on the matter, he replied, "If I was not too young to be in Christ, I was not too young to be at His table."[56]

Although Communions were primarily remembrance services, they were also occasions when the truths of the gospel were set before the people, leading often to deep conviction. McCheyne would have been in wholehearted agreement with the words of hymn writer Elizabeth R. Charles (1828–1896):

> No gospel like this feast,
> Spread for us, Lord, by Thee;
> No prophets or evangelists
> Preach the glad news more free.

At his second Communion in April 1840, he recorded in his diary:

> Mon. 20th—One (A.N.) was like a person struck through with a dart; she could neither stand nor go. Many were looking on her with faces of horror. Others were comforting her

---

54. Notes on young communicants, MACCH 1.7.
55. Andrew A. Bonar, *Memoir*, 124.
56. Van Valen, *Constrained by His Love*, 335.

in a very kind manner, bidding her to look to Jesus. Mr Burns went to the desk and told them of Kilsyth. Still they would not go away. Spoke a few words more to those around me, telling them of the loveliness of Christ, and the hardness of their hearts, that they could be so unmoved when one was so deeply wounded. The sobbing soon spread, till many heads were bent down, and the church was filled with sobbing. Many whom I did not know were now affected. After prayer, we dismissed near midnight. Many followed us. One, in great agony, prayed that she might find Christ that very night. So ends this blessed season.[57]

That same year McCheyne published his tract "This Do in Remembrance of Me" for his own flock first of all. He addressed the congregation of St. Peter's in these words in October 1841:

I fear the Lord's Supper is profaned in a dreadful manner among you. Many come who are living in positive sins, or in the neglect of positive duties. Many come who know that they were never converted; many who in their hearts ridicule the very thought of conversion. Unworthy communicating is a fearful sin; on account of it God is greatly provoked to withdraw His Spirit from you, to visit you with frowns of providence, and to seal you to the day of perdition.... Deal honestly with your soul, and pray over what I am now writing; and may He who opened the heart of Lydia open your heart (while I explain).[58]

Fencing the tables was as essential after the revival as before it. Before his first Communion in 1840, for example, having preached the action sermon on John 17:24, McCheyne fenced the table from Acts 5:3, "Lying to the Holy Ghost."[59]

---

57. Andrew A. Bonar, *Memoir*, 128.

58. Andrew A. Bonar, *Memoir*, 569 (full text, 569–76).

59. Andrew A. Bonar, *Memoir*, 127. McCheyne wrote in his diary on January 19, 1840: "Felt great help in fencing the tables from Acts V. 3: 'Lying to the Holy Ghost.' Came down and served the first table with much more calmness and collectedness than ever I remember to have enjoyed" (full text, 173–75).

## Exhorting Christians to Persevere in the Faith

Although he had written to his sister, Eliza, that "the greatest change of all is upon the Christians,"[60] he did find it needful to exhort them to greater dedication in the Lord's service. Taking as his text on one occasion the commendation of Caleb in Numbers 14:24, he delivered a sermon titled "Follow the Lord Fully." Because of his own constant self-reformation he was well entitled to say this: "You must follow him without any inconsistency...and without any delay, you must give yourself away to him. You must give away your understanding, will and affections; your body and all its members, your eyes and tongue, your hands and feet. So that you are in no respect your own, but his alone.... This is to follow the Lord fully."[61]

In a sermon preached on Romans 13:11 ("Now it is high time to awake out of sleep: for now is our salvation nearer than when we believed"), McCheyne said he feared "there are many sleeping Christians among you." He compared his listeners to the people in Ephesus, those who "have forgotten the fresh grasp of a Savior."[62]

On another occasion he sought in a sermon on Hosea 7:9 to arouse those who were not making progress in spiritual things. His words show that just as he was never complacent or satisfied with his own spiritual condition, so he also tried to awaken professing Christians to a realization of how far some of them had slipped:

> How many have lost their relish for the house of God! It is not with you as in months past. The Thursday evening is not so prized as once it was, the private prayer-meeting is seldom if ever visited, the company of Christ more lightly esteemed. Is there not less zeal for the conversion of others, less prayer, less praise, less liberality? Ah! Brethren, we as a congregation are a monument that there is such a thing as spiritual decay!... On many of your hearts I fear we must write, "Ichabod. The glory is departed"!

---

60. McCheyne to Eliza, December 31, 1839, MACCH 2.1.91.

61. McCheyne, *From the Preacher's Heart*, 379 (full text, 374–82). Sermon preached in Dundee in 1842.

62. McCheyne, *Basket of Fragments*, 181–87. Sermon preached April 2, 1840.

He then went on to spell out various marks of declension: the Bible neglected, prayer neglected, Christ little esteemed, sin not hated, Christians lightly esteemed, the ungodly not warned, lust allowed to prevail, and worldly company.[63]

Much of McCheyne's time was taken up with seeking to help those who were truly the Lord's to grow in grace. He linked the low state of some Christians to the fact that so much time had to be spent addressing the unsaved: "So much time and labour has to be expended on the barren fig trees, that the precious vines are left unprotected and uncultivated."[64]

During his few years in Dundee, McCheyne had always taken a keen interest in the religious life of the town, as well as being the recognized leader, along with Roxburgh, of the evangelicals in the presbytery (see appendix 1 for details).

## An Increasingly Judgmental Tone

In the last year of his life, McCheyne's preaching took on a more judgmental tone. This may have been partly because he was conscious that his life was fast coming to an end. For example, early in 1843, he addressed these words to his congregation: "I do not expect to live long. I expect a sudden call some day—perhaps soon, and therefore I speak very plainly.... Changes are coming; every eye before me shall soon be dim in death. Another pastor shall feed this flock; another singer lead the psalm; another flock shall fill this fold."[65]

As he touched on eternal punishment, however, he always did so with great compassion. As early as November 1835, just after he began as assistant to Reverend John Bonar at Larbert and Dunipace, in a sermon on Malachi 1:6, he said, under his heading "Earthly Virtues May Accompany a Man to Hell," "I desire to speak with all reverence and with all tenderness upon so dreadful a subject. The man who speaks

---

63. McCheyne, *Basket of Fragments*, 417–22.

64. McCheyne, *Basket of Fragments*, 437–38 (full text, 435–43). The sermon was on Zechariah 8:13: "The Believer a Blessing—the Unbeliever a Curse."

65. Andrew A. Bonar, *Memoir*, 159.

of hell should do so with tears in his eyes."[66] The following year, while conversing with his close friend Andrew Bonar and learning that the latter had preached on the text "The wicked shall be turned into hell," McCheyne asked him, "Were you able to preach it *with tenderness*?"[67]

On January 15, 1842, McCheyne took up the theme of castaway from 1 Corinthians 9:27 and preached that Sabbath morning on the mental agonies of hell. He told the congregation that they would remember in a lost eternity their misspent Sabbaths, their lying lips, and all the entreaties of their minister that went unheeded. Then they would know what it is to be a castaway.[68]

In July 1842, McCheyne preached on Mark 9:44, "Where their worm dieth not, and the fire is not quenched." He urged his hearers to flee from the wrath to come. They should search the Scriptures to see the truth of an eternal hell. He then referred to those who spoke on hell—David, Paul, John, the Lord Jesus—all doing so because it is all true. At the end of his sermon, having spoken first, as he had so often done, to believers, then to those seeking Christ anxiously, he addressed himself finally to the unconverted:

> Ah! You are fools and you think you are wise; but O I beseech you, search the Scriptures. Do not take my word about an eternal hell; it is the testimony of God, when He spoke about it. O if it be true—if there be a furnace of fire—if there be a second death, if it is not annihilation, but an eternal hell—O is it reasonable to go on living in sin? You think you are wise— that you are no fanatic—that you are no hypocrite; but you will soon gnash your teeth in pain; it will come; and the bitter- est thought will be, that you heard about hell, and yet rejected Christ. O then, turn ye, turn ye, why will ye die?[69]

As the year ended, McCheyne preached two sermons on con- secutive weeks, one titled "God's Rectitude in Future Punishment"

---

66. McCheyne, *From the Preacher's Heart*, 35 (full text, 29–36).

67. Andrew A. Bonar, *Memoir*, 43. McCheyne recorded this in his diary on June 15, 1836.

68. McCheyne, *Basket of Fragments*, 172–73 (full text, 168–73).

69. McCheyne, *Basket of Fragments*, 154–55 (full text, 148–55).

(Ps. 11:6–7), and the other, "The Eternal Torment of the Wicked" (Rev. 19:3).[70] There was no build-up to Christmas in those days! One of his last two discourses, published shortly after his death, was on Romans 9:22–23, "The Vessels of Wrath Fitted to Destruction." In it he said, "One reason why there are vessels of wrath fitted to destruction is, that God may show by contrast the riches of His grace on the vessels of mercy." For the very destruction of the wicked makes known the riches of divine grace.[71] McCheyne always felt he was preaching as a witness to the righteousness of God.

In the last year or so of his life, McCheyne was increasingly pre-occupied with the ecclesiastical issues of the day, whether the mission to the Jews, the church extension scheme, or his attendance at the various meetings that led eventually to the setting up of the Free Church. Robertson characterized this time thus: "There was a sense also in which McCheyne became a little more detached and national in his ministry. This was partly because his concern was national if not international."[72] It grieved him to see whole areas of the country still not as yet enjoying an evangelical ministry because of the lingering effects of Moderatism. Therefore, even during the course of the revival he would take off to preach in such areas. One gets the distinct impression that, had the railway network been further developed when he ministered, he would have availed himself of this for longer journeys more often, and his beloved mare, Tully, would have been left in the stable. Burns also indulged in periodic preaching trips.[73]

---

70. McCheyne, *Basket of Fragments*, 155–61, 162–67.

71. R. M. McCheyne, *The Eternal Inheritance the Believer's Portion, and The Vessels of Wrath Fitted to Destruction; being the Substance of the Two Last Discourses preached in St. Peter's Church, Dundee, Sabbath, March 12, 1843* (Dundee, Scotland: William Middleton, 1843), 18–31.

72. Robertson, *Awakening*, 172.

73. Even during the revival year, Burns could not resist occasional evangelistic excursions. Instead of returning to Dundee after the Kilsyth Communion, he went to Paisley to preach in the High church there. In September he was preaching in Kirkintilloch and Denny. In October he was in Edinburgh at St. George's Church, also visiting the Orphan Hospital, which Whitefield had lent his support to a century earlier. The following month he was preaching in the Secession church in St. Andrews. Islay Burns, *Memoir*, 124–27.

The periodic absence of McCheyne and Burns, however, showed that the progress of the revival was not dependent on the continued presence of either of them, with able ministers like Roxburgh, Lewis, Cumming, and others to assist.

## Pastor or Evangelist?

In his memoir, Bonar touched upon the dilemma that McCheyne seemed to be wrestling with: "Many of us thought that he afterwards erred in the abundant frequency of his evangelistic labours at a time when he was still bound to a particular flock."[74] It was partly the lingering influence of Moderatism that led McCheyne to suggest that men should be ordained as evangelists, "with full power to preach in every pulpit of their district,—faithful, judicious, lively preachers, who may go from parish to parish, and thus carry life into many a dead corner."[75] Bonar, on his part, saw McCheyne had such a passion for souls, and he believed the Lord would call him out to "evangelistic more than pastoral labours."[76] In a letter to his sister, Eliza, McCheyne confided, "I think God will yet make me a wandering minister. My nature inclines thereto."[77] So deeply did he feel in this matter, that a friend relates of him, as they rode together through a parish where the pastor "clothed himself with the wool, but fed not the flock," he "raised his hand with vehemence as he spoke of the people left to perish under such a minister."[78] This was something that Burns and McCheyne had discussed after the latter's return from Palestine. Their continued correspondence also served to highlight the blessing that seemed to accompany Burns's itinerary.[79] In Decem-

---

74. Andrew A. Bonar, *Memoir*, 60.
75. Andrew A. Bonar, *Memoir*, 138.
76. Andrew A. Bonar, *Memoir*, 145.
77. Yeaworth, "Robert Murray McCheyne," 301.
78. Andrew A. Bonar, *Memoir*, 138.
79. For example, "The work of the Lord continues to deepen here. I had about 30 young men with me last night seeking conversation and prayer whose cases as far as I went in examination are very interesting and certainly the fruit of the present work." MACCH 2.4.7. "The work of the Lord appears to be prospering from day to day in Perth and the neighbourhood." MACCH 2.4.8. Burns wrote from Anstruther

ber 1842, Burns wrote to McCheyne from Largo manse in Fife to say that he had his hands more than full and was getting into many a Moderate pulpit: "You will wonder how I get in to such places, I wonder not less, but the hand of God is visible, opening the way through the wishes of the people." Then he pleaded the needs of Scotland for itinerant preachers:

> What are you thinking also in regard to a more general diffusion of the Gospel over the land by evangelistic labour? Is the Lord, do you think, preparing you for this either in outward circumstances or in inward bias? Whatever is to be done in this way—must it not be done speedily? For when ministers leave their churches especially in the country parts, we cannot hope that liberty will long be given to any of us to interfere with the peace—accursed peace, I fear—of their successors.

Burns was assured that he was doing the right thing with his itinerant work. He had more than he could cope with in Fife. He continued:

> Oh! that you and a few more of your brethren were sent forth by the Lord to the field in which I am favoured to be. The people are waiting in the market place until some one call them in the name of Jesus. Oh! the fields are white—why should St. Peter's or any other parish have shower upon shower when many districts have not a drop! The time is short: come away to the help of the Lord—the help of the Lord against the Mighty.[80]

McCheyne's preaching itinerary in his last few months suggests that it would not have taken much to launch him forth on a regular basis. He preached for his friend Bonar at Collace early in the year, then went to Lintrathen, where the folk would willingly put down

---

to say God was at work, as the dissenting bodies were shutting up their own buildings and meeting in his tent in the churchyard. MACCH 2.4.11. "I have for the last fortnight been meeting almost exclusively in school houses with the mill population and on some occasions, there seemed to be a very general, and in some cases I hope, a saving impression." MACCH 2.4.15.

80. Burns to McCheyne, December 16, 1842, MACCH 2.4.29.

their tools in the middle of the day if he would come and preach.[81] A few weeks later he proceeded to the districts of Deer and Ellon, refreshing an area long dominated by Moderatism. This, his last preaching tour, wore him out, no doubt contributing to weaken his resistance when he contracted typhus fever.

McCheyne's dilemma was never to be resolved before he was called home. He continued on in the pastorate at St. Peter's until strength failed him. The wholehearted commitment that had characterized his labors among the people, and which he sought to instill in them, is brought out in the closing words of his second lecture on the family at Bethany (John 11:5–10):

> Oh, that you who are believers would be persuaded to follow Jesus fearlessly wherever he calls you! If you are a believer, you will often be tempted to shrink back. The path of a Christian is narrow, and often difficult. But what have you to fear? Have you the blood of Christ upon your conscience, and the presence of God within your soul? Are there not twelve hours in the day? Are we not all immortal till our work is done?[82]

As McCheyne lay dying in March 1843, among his last words were these: "This parish, Lord, this people, this whole place!... Holy Father, keep through Thine own name those whom Thou hast given me."[83] McCheyne undoubtedly had a true pastor's heart and a deep burden for the town in which the Lord had placed him. Nevertheless, inasmuch as he found himself to be constantly preaching to a mixed congregation at St. Peter's, it could also be said that he fulfilled in a measure the injunction of the apostle Paul to Timothy in 2 Timothy 4:5: "Do the work of an evangelist, make full proof of thy ministry."

---

81. Andrew A. Bonar, *Memoir*, 159.
82. McCheyne, *From the Preacher's Heart*, 482 (full text, 477–82).
83. Andrew A. Bonar, *Memoir*, 163–64.

# 6

# McCheyne and the Lambs

On J.T., A Believing Boy, who died February 1842.

> I little thought, when last we met,
> Thy sun on earth was nearly set:
> I said what I can ne'er forget,
>   "Dear boy, we'll meet again."

> Though thou wert tossed upon thy bed,
> And sometimes criedst, "My head, my head!"
> Yet still the smile came back—I said,
>   "Fair boy, we'll meet again."

> No hope thy weeping mother had,
> Thy sister's face was pale and sad,
> But thine was always bright and glad—
>   Dear boy, we'll meet again.

> "Twas kind," thou saidst, "in God to die
> For worms like me. Once I would fly
> A darkened room—now Christ is nigh,"—
>   Fair boy, we'll meet again.

> "I love you well, my mother dear—
> I love you all, yet shed no tear—
> I'd rather be with Christ than here"—
>   Farewell, we'll meet again.

> "I fain would live to preach to men;
> But if my God should spare till then,

I would be loth to die again"—
   Dear boy, we'll meet again.

The Sabbath-sun rose bright and clear
When thine was setting on us here,
To shine more bright in yonder sphere—
   Farewell, we'll meet again.

I stood beside thy silent bed:
Thy marble brow was cold and dead,
Thy gentle soul was fled—was fled—
   Dear boy, we'll meet again.

I saw thee in thy narrow rest,
The clods upon thy coffin pressed;
The clouds dropped tears, yet in my breast
   God said, "We'll meet again."

Yes, parents, smile through all your tears;
A crown of life your darling wears;
The grave a shady porch appears,
   To where we'll meet again.

The precious dust beneath that lies,
Shall at the call of Jesus rise,
To meet the Bridegroom in the skies,
   That day we'll meet again.

These verses by McCheyne were written on the death of the younger son of a family he was well acquainted with, the Thains.[1] John Thain, a merchant and shipowner, lived in a country house called Heath Park in Blairgowrie. He was an elder in Robert MacDonald's church in Blairgowrie and for some time a trustee of St. Peter's Church. In the winter months the family made their home in Park Place, Dundee, attending St. Peter's, which was within walking distance. Heath Park became like a Bethany to McCheyne. He often visited there, benefiting

---

1. Andrew A. Bonar, *Memoir*, 647–48.

not only from the beauty and freshness of the Perthshire countryside but also from the spiritual fellowship and friendship of a home in which the fear of the Lord prevailed.[2]

The younger son, Johnnie, took ill late in 1841. A correspondence developed between him and McCheyne. The boy had written to him to say, "The Lord has thought it necessary to afflict me to try and bring me to Himself.... I feel I am a lost sinner, but Christ has said 'him that cometh to me I will in no wise cast out.' I would like to be His, to be saved in the Lord. O may the Lord bless this affliction to my soul and make me one of his lambs."[3]

McCheyne replied by expressing how dear the boy was to him, "because your soul is precious." He agreed with him about his affliction: "It is really for this that He smites you. His heart, His hand, and His rod, are all inscribed with love. But then, see that He does bring you to Himself." He went on to speak in uncompromising language of the lake of fire and brimstone stretching beneath every unrepentant sinner. He encouraged the boy by referring to a little girl of three or four years who approached him while he was preaching in Perth the previous Sabbath, desperate to be saved: "Her mother said she had been crying the whole night about her soul, and would take no comfort till she should find Jesus." McCheyne paid several visits to Johnnie. He wrote to his older brother, Alexander, some time later to say he was quite sure of the young lad's salvation:

> I do trust and believe that he was a saved boy. You know I am rather slow of coming to this conviction, and not fond of speaking when I have not good evidence; but here, I think, God has not left us in any doubt.... Over and over he told me that he was not afraid to die, for Christ had died. "How kind

---

2. William Norrie, comp., *Dundee Celebrities of the Nineteenth Century...* (Dundee, Scotland: William Norrie, 270–71; Van Valen, *Constrained by His Love*, 250. Thain was active in civic and religious activities in the area. He was a member of the Dundee town council. He was a keen supporter of Non-Intrusion and the Anti-Patronage Parties. In 1843 he joined the Free Church and was often a member of the presbytery.

3. Johnnie Thain to McCheyne, January 21, 1842, MACCH 2.3.3.

it was in God to send Jesus to die for sinners.".... He is not lost,
but is gone before.... I was at your house on Sabbath night,
and saw them all,—sorrowful, yet rejoicing. Your dear little
brother lies like a marble statue in the peaceful sleep of death,
till Jesus' voice shall waken him.[4]

## Motivations for Ministering to the Young

McCheyne did not spend time writing to and visiting with this young
lad simply because he was a friend of the family. His love for young
people was motivated by two factors. First, there was the brevity of
life. A good percentage of the people of Dundee never made it beyond
twenty years of age. Early in 1837, as he was getting to know the people with his systematic visitation, influenza was raging. The brevity of
life was brought home to him: "Did I tell you of the boy I was asked to
see on Sabbath evening, just when I got myself comfortably seated at
home? I went, and was speaking to him of the freeness and fullness of
Jesus, when he gasped a little and died."[5]

Second, McCheyne was fully persuaded that the young could
believe and be saved. To those who objected that some biblical doctrines were too difficult for a child to understand, his reply was, "God
can convert and edify a child with the same ease with which He can
change the heart of a grown man." Grace can enable a child to "understand and relish divine things as fully as those of mature age."[6] In this
respect the other evangelical ministers of the area were at one with
McCheyne. When replying to the last of the questions the Aberdeen
Presbytery put to him regarding the revival concerning the children
who professed to be saved, he graciously included his colleagues in
other churches in his reply: "The ministers engaged in the work of
God in this place, believing that children are lost, and may through
grace be saved, have therefore spoken to children as freely as to grown
persons, and God has so greatly honoured their labours, that many

---

4. R. M. McCheyne, *Letters to Inquirers and Young Converts* (Edinburgh: William Oliphant, 1875), 31–35; Andrew A. Bonar, *Memoir,* 311–12.

5. Andrew A. Bonar, *Memoir,* 57.

6. Andrew A. Bonar, *Memoir,* 568.

children, from ten years old and upwards, have given full evidence of their being born again."[7]

One of his favorite authors was Jonathan Edwards. McCheyne pointed to the evidence of the revival in Northampton and neighboring counties of New England in 1735. In his *Narrative of Surprising Conversions*, Edwards referred to thirty converts between ages ten and fourteen, two between nine and ten, and one of about four years of age.[8]

## Schools for the Young

It will be remembered that the task of the first minister at St. Peter's was "to excavate a congregation for himself from the surrounding district."[9] It was necessary for McCheyne, once in post, to develop work among the young people. He gained great encouragement here from a visit to Blairgowrie, where he attended an impressive meeting at Robert MacDonald's church. He wrote to his parents of more than four hundred young people present, with their teachers. The age range was from six up to twenty-five. Everything was done decently and in order. They sang psalms, ate a communal meal, and listened to various ministers giving short addresses, including McCheyne speaking on Jesus's love to little children. He concluded his letter by remarking:

> But there was so much variety and excellent entertainment both for soul and body that I am sure nobody wearied, not even the youngest children. I never did see so pleasing a sight. I do not remember ever spending a happier evening. Indeed many things made the tears come to my eyes. I hope also some good was done. If God command the blessing even life for evermore. Remember Blairgowrie has been long a dead sea. Never anything like this heard within its borders. And

---

7. Andrew A. Bonar, *Memoir*, 550–51.

8. Jonathan Edwards, *A Faithful Narrative of Surprising Conversions*, in *The Works of Jonathan Edwards*, ed. Edward Hickman (Edinburgh: Banner of Truth Trust, 1976), 1:350.

9. Managers' Minutes of St. Peter's Church.

Handsel Monday used to be spent in nothing but drinking. I wish we could have something as good in poor Dundee.[10]

Just before this visit, he had made a beginning with the setting up of Sabbath schools. It was pioneering work. In his report to the Aberdeen Presbytery in March 1841, he said he found it impossible to establish schools to start with, "while very lately there were instituted with ease nineteen such schools that are well taught and well attended."[11] McCheyne took a keen interest in the education of children not only in his own parish but also in the presbytery. Because he believed that the primary purpose of a school was to convert a child, he supervised the selection and training of teachers. He even wrote some notes for them. When inspected, St. Peter's school was found by the presbytery to be "well and cheerfully taught, particularly considering the great numbers attending."[12] As teachers were found, a network of schools was established, the average attendance in 1839 being 150. Sabbath school superintendent Edward Caird wrote to McCheyne in Edinburgh not long before he left for Palestine, describing the older boys as "still very wild." The teachers would put up with them that they might be instructed: "Who knows but the Lord in bringing them to us may have a great work of mercy and love in store for the very roughest homes among them."[13] Not content with his own parish, McCheyne visited a school in St. George's Parish

---

10. McCheyne to Papa and Mamma, January 19, 1838, MACCH 2.1.34. Handsel Monday was a secular holiday on the first Monday of January. It was a time of giving good luck gifts but could degenerate into a time of drinking. It was later replaced by Boxing Day.

11. Andrew A. Bonar, *Memoir*, 547.

12. *Dundee, Perth, and Cupar Advertiser*, February 3, 1842; D. B. Mellis, appraisal of St. Peter's, MACCH, 1.13, 1841; and Andrew A. Bonar, *Memoir*, 62.

13. Edward Caird to McCheyne, March 12, 1839, MACCH 2.1.70. In "Death's Lessons," a sermon on Job 14:1–2, under the third heading, "Learn to Seek One Another's Souls," McCheyne said to teachers: "Dear teachers! Teach the children plainly, for children die. Do not mind their impatience and waywardness. Remember they are dying children—Death's mark is on them. The forester puts a mark round the trees that are to be cut down. Every child has got Death's mark." McCheyne, *From the Preacher's Heart*, 350.

"and preached to many weeping children."[14] He recorded in his diary his impressions after one visit to a school: "Had considerable joy in teaching the children. Oh, for real heart work among them." Bonar remarked that he could accommodate himself to their level, using his talents to keep their attention. He did this because "he regarded the soul of a child as infinitely precious."[15]

## Preaching Directly to the Young

In addition to setting up schools, McCheyne sought to win the young to Christ through his preaching, his visitation, and his writing. In the sermon "The Saviour's Tears over the Lost," from Luke 19:41–42, he emphasized how crucial it was to seek the Lord while young in years:

> The Time of Youth. I do not pretend to give a reason why it is so; but God has so ordered it in his infinite wisdom, that the period of youth is the best time for being saved. It has been observed, and it is very remarkable, that in all the great revivals that have taken place in our own and in bygone days, the most of those that have been converted were young people. Jonathan Edwards states this in his revival in New England, and Robe states the same in his account of the revival in Kilsyth in 1742. And have we not seen it among ourselves, that while young persons have been melted and converted, those who are older have only grown more hardened in sin. O young people! Improve, I entreat you, your young days. Seek the Lord while yet your hearts are young and tender. If you delay, you will grow harder, and then, humanly speaking, it will be more difficult to be saved. No doubt God can save sinners at any age; but he seems peculiarly to choose the time of youth. He loves to hear an infant sing—he loves to hear praise from the mouths of babes and sucklings. Oh then, my brethren, will you not seek him in the days of your youth? Will you not call upon him while he may be found? If you let your young days pass over your heads without being saved, you will

---

14. Horatius Bonar, *Life of the Rev. John Milne*, 33.
15. Andrew A. Bonar, *Memoir*, 61.

remember your misspent privileges when you are in hell, and you will bitterly mourn over them throughout all eternity.[16]

In a message preached from Psalm 90:14, "O Satisfy Us Early with Thy Mercy," he said, "A full close with Christ in early life is the greatest of all blessings." He pointed out to his listeners that it was the experience of all ministers in all the Scottish revivals that most believers are converted while they are young, and few people are converted past middle age. He cautioned his young hearers about the brevity of life. Referring to his text he remarked: "It was this that drew out the prayer of the text. They saw their fathers falling in the wilderness thousands in a day." He ended by referring to the uncertainty of life and the happiness of being early brought to Christ, "that we may rejoice all our days."[17] On another occasion, preaching from Matthew 9:35–38, on Christ's compassion on the multitudes as sheep having no shepherd, he said to the youngsters at St. Peter's, "Little children, if you would take Jesus for a Savior, then you might carry all your griefs to him; for Jesus knows what it is to be a little child."[18]

## Admonishing Parents Not to Neglect Their Children

As well as addressing children frankly in his sermons, McCheyne spoke pointedly to parents: "Parents! Seek your children's souls from infancy. Pray for them before they are born. Travail in birth with them till Christ be formed in them. Do not say they are too young and cannot understand. God can teach babes. Oh if you neglect this, will you not regret it when the green sod lies on their breasts?"[19]

In one of his sermons on the righteousness of God, from Romans 10:3, preached at Larbert, Dunipace, and Dundee, and perhaps on other occasions elsewhere, McCheyne emphasized the duty of parents to instruct their children. While they themselves could not turn

---

16. McCheyne, *Basket of Fragments*, 94. Preached at his Thursday evening class, December 31, 1841.

17. Sermons 1837–1838, 1:313, MACCH 1.1.

18. McCheyne, *From the Preacher's Heart*, 162. Preached November 12, 1837.

19. McCheyne, *From the Preacher's Heart*, 350.

the hearts of the children, they ought to lay the truth before them, by means of which their hearts may be turned to the Lord:

> If you will have no mercy on your own souls—will you have no mercy on the souls of your children—if you will not yourselves seek to have the veil of your own ignorance taken away.... Will you dare to heap upon your souls the everlasting curses of your children by keeping them back from gaining that knowledge which alone can save their soul? Will not the ordinary pains of hell be bad enough but will you also draw down the deeper agonies that await the souls of your children?[20]

## Visiting the Young

Just as visitation was the essential accompaniment to his preaching, so McCheyne was not content that the young be taught formally in schools. He would spend time visiting the young. Johnnie Thain was no exception. In one of his visitation notebooks, there is reference to a family of Seceders in the area. He was visiting their little boy of eight or nine (the parents were a godly couple), who, he wrote, "loves me to come and see him. Loved to hear of Christ.... He was willing to take Christ as his surety." McCheyne spoke words of comfort and encouragement to the parents when little James McKechnie died: "Not lost but gone before. May we tread in his steps. Dear child may our end like thine be peace."[21] In the same notebook, his conversation with a twelve-year-old girl, entered simply as "M. M.," shows the care he took to get the young properly rooted and grounded in the faith. He discussed such matters with her as concern for her soul, how precious Christ was to her, and the attraction of the world. He pointed her to Christ as her strength and also sought to correct her approach to reading her Bible: "Showed her my way of reading, marking verses and praying over them."[22]

---

20. Sermon on Romans 10, verse 3, Dundee City Archives, MS TD 87/1.
21. Dundee visitation, 1838, MACCH 1.14.
22. Dundee visitation, 1836–1838, MACCH 1.14.

Another youngster whom McCheyne and other ministers spent considerable time visiting was James Laing. He went to be with Christ in June 1842, aged thirteen years, after a protracted illness, having shown evidence of remarkable spiritual maturity in a boy so young. His testimony was published as "Another Lily Gathered." McCheyne used Laing's short life to show how the Spirit strives even with young children: "And when they grieve Him, and resist His awakening hand, He suffers long with them." James first showed some concern for his soul in the autumn of 1839, when the awakening began. At times he seemed under conviction, and then it would pass. In late October his health deteriorated. McCheyne visited him: "On the Saturday I paid a visit to their humble cottage, and found the little sufferer sitting by the fire. He began to weep bitterly while I spoke to him of Jesus having come into the world to save sinners. I was enabled in a simple manner to answer the objections that sinners make to an immediate closing with Christ."

Later that night he asked, "Have I only to believe that Jesus died for sinners? Is that all?" He was told yes. "Well I believe that Jesus died for me, for I am a poor, hell-deserving sinner. I have been praying all this afternoon, that when Jesus shed his blood for sinners, He would sprinkle some of it upon me, and He did it." He then read from Romans 5:8, "While we were yet sinners, Christ died for us." "I am not afraid to die now for Jesus died for me."

Thereafter McCheyne visited James regularly and would expound portions of Scripture to him: "A pious expression and a fervent prayer are not enough to feed the soul that is passing through the dark valley. Surely if sound and spiritual nourishment is needed by the soul at any time, it is in such an hour, when Satan uses all his arts to disturb and destroy." At this point McCheyne was assisted in visitation by Cumming of Dunbarney, Miller of Wallacetown, and Bonar of Collace. McCheyne commented: "I never met with any boy who had so clear a discovery of the way of pardon and acceptance through the doing and dying of the Lord Jesus, laid to our account."

One of the clear evidences of James's salvation could be seen in his concern for his young peers. After McCheyne had spoken to the

Sabbath scholars about him, they all came to visit him in his cottage. He witnessed to them all. "I have sinned with you; now I would like you to come to Christ with me." "Go and tell Jesus that you are poor, lost, hell-deserving sinners, and tell Him to give you a new heart. Mind, He's willing, and, oh, be earnest!—ye'll no get it unless ye be earnest."

Though in great weakness and pain, James spent much time in secret prayer. In the latter part of his illness, he was instrumental in awakening another boy, David, who had been quite wild. This David came three times a day to seek the prayers and counsel of his young instructor, until James's strength so declined he could no longer speak. The day before he died, David came in to see him. Looking straight at him, James said, "Seek on, David."

At the conclusion of this printed testimony, McCheyne drew some lessons. His first was for children: "You see here that you are not too young to have the Holy Spirit striving with you. You are not too young to resist the Holy Ghost. You are not too young to be converted and brought to Christ." He then addressed parents. In seeking the salvation of their children, they should not neglect the family altar: "Seek their conversion now, if you would meet them in glory hereafter. How will you bear to hear their young voices in the judgment, saying 'this father never prayed for me; this mother never warned me to flee from the wrath to come'? " He ended by addressing fellow ministers and Sabbath school workers, exhorting them to be more earnest in their efforts to secure the salvation of little children: "We have here one bright example more in addition to all those who have been recorded before, that God can convert and edify a child with the same ease with which He can change the heart of a grown man."[23]

## Writing for the Young

Writing was, in fact, a natural way for McCheyne to communicate his concerns for the young and to seek for their salvation. He wrote several tracts specifically for them. One such was "Reasons Why Chil-

---

23. Diary, 1839–1842, MACCH 1.8; Andrew A. Bonar, *Memoir*, 551–68.

dren Should Flee to Christ without Delay," produced at the beginning of 1839. In it he sought to bring before children that which they would not normally think of at their young age—that no one has any guarantee of tomorrow: "How many friends have you lying in the grave! Some of you have more friends in the grave than in this world. They were carried away 'as with a flood,' and we are hastening after them.... It is an absolute certainty that, in a few years, all of you who read this will be lying in the grave. Oh, what need, then, to fly to Christ without delay!"[24]

Even while McCheyne was apart from them, on his trip to Palestine, his burden for the young found expression. In his ninth pastoral letter, from Leghorn, he wrote home on May 2, 1839: "My dear children in the Sabbath schools I always think upon on the Sabbath evenings, and on those who patiently labour among them. The Lord Himself give you encouragement, and a full reward."[25] During a short time away from Dundee, assisting Horatius Bonar at Kelso at the Communion season, he again laid bare his heart with regard to the young:

> You cannot tell what a sweet comfort it is to me when I am so far distant from my flock to know that you are in the midst of the lambs speaking to God for them and speaking to them from God.... Do not be impatient—wait on the Lord. The blessing will come. Use a few spare half hours in seeking after the lambs on the week days. This will prove to the parents that you are in earnest. To bring one child to the bosom of Christ would be reward for all our pains in Eternity. Oh with what glowing hearts we shall meet in heaven those whom God has used us as humble instruments in saving.[26]

McCheyne also used his poetic gift to express simple gospel truths. For example, "Oil in the Lamp," based on the parable of the ten virgins in Matthew 25:1–13, was written to help a class of Sabbath

---

24. Andrew A. Bonar, *Memoir*, 585–86.
25. Andrew A. Bonar, *Memoir*, 255.
26. McCheyne to his home fellowship, February 24, 1841, MACCH 2.7.15.

scholars in 1841. Having explained the meaning of the verses, the importance of seeking the Lord while He may be found, he stressed the danger of leaving it too late at the end:

> Sinners! Behold the gate
> Of Jesus open still;
> Come, ere it be too late,
> And enter if you will.
>
> The Savior's gentle hand
> Knocks at your door to-day;
> But vain His loud demand—
> You spurn His love away.
>
> So at the Savior's door
> You'll knock, with trembling heart:
> The day of mercy o'er,
> Jesus will say—Depart.[27]

In "The Child Coming to Jesus," written in July 1841, McCheyne pictured a young child appealing to mother, father, sisters, and friends not to hold him back from fully trusting in Christ. He concluded with:

> Loving playmates, gay and smiling,
> Bid me not forsake the cross,
> Hard to bear is your reviling,
> Yet for Jesus all is dross.
>
> Yea, though all the world have chid me,
> Father, Mother, sister, friend—
> Jesus never will forbid me!
> Jesus loves me to the end!
>
> Gentle Shepherd, on thy shoulder
> Carry me, a sinful lamb;
> Give me faith, and make me bolder,
> Till with Thee in heaven I am.[28]

---

27. Andrew A. Bonar, *Memoir*, 645–47. The last three of sixteen stanzas.
28. Andrew A. Bonar, *Memoir*, 644–45.

McCheyne took every opportunity to witness to the young. In a book he sent to a little boy of his congregation, he could not resist inserting some lines in the flyleaf to encourage his study of the Bible and to seek the Lord while young in years.[29] On another occasion, he put a simple question to one boy whom he encountered playing in the street: "Walter, do you love your soul?" The boy did not respond at the time, but the words had actually sunk deep and remained with him. Some years later he got saved and became, as Reverend Walter Davidson, the minister of Knox Free Church in Perth.[30]

### Young People's Response to McCheyne

The love, affection, and concern that McCheyne had shown to the young were certainly reciprocated, and his effort was well expended. In his absence, they showed concern for their pastor as he recuperated in Edinburgh. In January 1839, one of his parishioners, Mrs. Likely, wrote to him in connection with the Sabbath school: "I only mention how affecting it is to see our dear little scholars waiting with tears in their eyes to hear you prayed for.... Our weekly prayer meeting never was so well filled as it is now."[31] On the eve of his return to Dundee in November 1839, Bonar recorded a packed church building, with "passages...completely filled, and the stairs to the pulpit crowded, on the one side with the aged, on the other with eagerly-listening children."[32]

It was previously noted that in McCheyne's absence, the number of prayer meetings had grown to thirty-nine, five of them being attended and conducted entirely by children. J. C. Smith, a youngster at the time, looking back on those revival days, commented, "It seemed to be natural for us and delightful to go here and there to the meetings, to sing and pray and read the Bible."[33] These meetings were

---

29. Andrew A. Bonar, *Memoir*, 61–62.

30. John MacPherson, *Revival and Revival Work: A Record of the Labours of D. L. Moody and Ira D. Sankey, and Other Evangelists* (London: Morgan and Scott, 1875), 21; Van Valen, *Constrained by His Love*, 185.

31. Mrs. Likely to McCheyne, January 29, 1839, MACCH 2.1.51.

32. Andrew A. Bonar, *Memoir*, 135.

33. J. C. Smith, *Robert Murray McCheyne* (London: Elliot Stock, 1910), 62.

not by any means confined to St. Peter's. A number of boys who went to St. David's Church met for prayer in a factory early on Sabbath morning to ask for the Lord's blessing on the work of the day.[34] Some of the Dundee children who were holding prayer meetings showed a fair degree of spiritual maturity. They wrote letters of encouragement to those of their own age in Kilsyth who were similarly caught up in the revival there.[35]

## Many Young People Converted

What must have brought joy to the heart of McCheyne was the number of young people converted. MacPherson stated, "A great measure of the success of the awakening generally as well as in Dundee, was with the young people."[36] The blessing had begun under Burns. As early as August 23 he met with twenty-two people, who were "under soul distress…among whom were two girls about nine and a boy of eleven."[37]

As a picture emerged, McCheyne was able to write in his notebook that "the number of little children saved is quite remarkable."[38] To his friend Andrew Bonar, he wrote as early as December 2, 1839: "One, eleven years old, is a singular instance of Divine Grace. When asked if she desired to be made holy, she said, 'Indeed, I often wish I was awa' that I might sin nae mair!' A lad of fifteen is a fine tender-hearted believer. W.S., ten, is also a happy boy."[39] To his family he wrote, "Many of the little children are wonderful monuments of grace."[40]

All this had resulted without any special children's meetings being held. This was actually a question put to McCheyne by the Aberdeen

---

34. Smith, *Robert Murray McCheyne*, 214.

35. Smith, *Robert Murray McCheyne*, 53.

36. MacPherson, *Revival and Revival Work*, 310.

37. Harry Sprange, *Children in Revival: 300 Years of God's Work in Scotland* (Fearn, Scotland: Christian Focus, 2002), 78; Kennedy, *Apostle of the North*, 230.

38. Notebook, 102, MACCH 1.10.

39. Andrew A. Bonar, *Memoir*, 118.

40. McCheyne to family in Edinburgh, December 9, 1839, MACCH 2.1.85.

Presbytery, to which he replied, "I am not aware of any meetings that have been held peculiarly for children with the exception of the Sabbath school, the children's prayer meetings and a sermon to children on the Monday evening after communion. It was commonly at the public meetings in the house of God that children were impressed, often also in their own little meetings, when no minister was present." He emphasized that his colleagues in the ministry, like himself, spoke as freely to the children as to the adults in the congregation, "and God has so greatly honoured their labours."[41]

As a direct result of the first part of the awakening in St. Peter's, nine children from ages ten to sixteen applied to take Communion.[42] In April 1840, of the thirty candidates who presented themselves for church membership, and of the same number for several Communions thereafter, a significant number were teenagers. Requests for admission to the Lord's Table among the young were noticeable.[43]

It is perhaps fitting, because of McCheyne's great love for the young and his interest in their eternal welfare, that his last impromptu "sermon" should have been addressed to a few of the lambs. Even while the fever was setting in, he was performing one last pastoral duty—joining two of his flock in marriage.[44] At the conclusion of this, a lady who was far from sympathetic to him sought to make fun of him. Reverend McGillivray, who was present, described the incident. She sent a little girl across the room with a flower and a favor for him:

Will 'oo put this in 'oor coat?"
"O yes, my dear," he answered, "but you must help me." And so the child did, fastening the flower into his button-hole, and pinning the favor on his coat. "Now," he said, "I have done what you wished; will you do what I would like?"
"Yes," she replied.

---

41. Andrew A. Bonar, *Memoir*, 550–51.
42. Andrew A. Bonar, *Memoir*, 124.
43. Andrew A. Bonar, *Memoir*, 126–27; Van Valen, *Constrained by His Love*, 333–34; and Robertson, *Awakening*, 170.
44. Andrew A. Bonar, *Memoir*, 162.

"Well, I wish you to listen to the story of the Good Shepherd, who gave Himself for the sheep." As he was talking, five or six other young people gathered round, pressing as near to him as they could; and he spoke as tellingly, as wooingly, as ever he had done from his pulpit. Then he turned to his friend and said, "I feel such a pressure on my brow."[45]

This was his last unrehearsed address. The day after McCheyne's death, William Lamb recorded in his diary how he departed from the normal Sabbath school lesson for that evening. Instead, he read to his scholars McCheyne's address "To the Lambs of the Flock," which had been published the year before.[46] He spoke a few words with reference to the author's death. Many of the children were in tears. He wrote of the occasion, "I could not help mingling tears with my first prayers for these 'lambs' of the flock of our dear, departed pastor, who so carefully tended them and loved them. Oh that his prayers for them might be answered, even this night! I felt much enabled to pray earnestly for this."[47]

A week or so later, Lamb took with him to the Sabbath school Alexander Gatherer, McCheyne's assistant. Lamb read from another of McCheyne's tracts—"Reasons Why Children Should Flee to Christ." Gatherer also addressed them. The older scholars in particular seemed a good deal impressed. Lamb concluded, "Oh that some may this night have fled to Jesus Christ!"[48]

---

45. Smellie, *Robert Murray McCheyne*, 159–60.
46. Andrew A. Bonar, *Memoir*, 612–18.
47. Lamb, *McCheyne from the Pew*, 153.
48. Lamb, *McCheyne from the Pew*, 156–57.

# 7

# Responses to the Revival:
# Opposition and Approbation

The term Revival can be applied to the revitalization of a body which once possessed spiritual life, but which has lost its former vigour. "Revival" in this sense presumes that there already has been some degree of vitality in the body. Thus, Christian believers in a church may be stimulated in such a way that their new, reinforced commitment to Christ begins to energise the church in a dramatic fashion, leading to a deeper concern for the unconverted, and spilling out into the community, with the result that spiritual concern is aroused widely, and people who have been "awakened" seek spiritual counsel.

The second definition of "revival," as a movement which "awakens" the unregenerate to a sense of sin and spiritual lostness, is the best known application of the word. In this context, the term is imprecisely used in English, since the unregenerate possess no earlier spiritual vitality.

—Donald E. Meek, *Dictionary of Scottish
Church History and Theology*

Never, perhaps, was there one placed in better circumstances for testing the revival impartially, and seldom has any revival been more fully tested. He came among a people whose previous character he knew; he found a work wrought among them during his absence, in which he had not had any direct share; he returned home to go in and out among them, and to be a close observer of all that had taken place; and after a faithful and prayerful examination, he did most unhesitatingly say that the Lord had wrought great things, whereof he was glad;

and in the case of many of those whose souls were saved in that revival, he discovered remarkable answers to the prayers of himself, and of those who had come to the truth, before he left them.

> —Andrew A. Bonar, *Memoir and Remains of the Rev. Robert Murray McCheyne*

Several natural factors can tend to turn people's attention to spiritual matters and concern for their souls. These would include, as we have seen in chapter 1, such matters as the poverty, overcrowding, unemployment, disease, and short life span that affected so much of the fast-growing population of Dundee. This could provide fertile ground for the good seed of the Word.

## Revival Is a Divine Thing

Revival is a putting forth of divine strength. It is God visiting His people. Each revival in the history of Israel came when religion was at low ebb.[1] The revivals throughout the history of Christianity have tended to come when the spiritual life of a community or country was low and the preaching of the gospel was greatly neglected. One feature that stands out prominently in a time of revival is the sovereignty of God. A revival is the supreme manifestation of God's sovereignty. It happens in God's own time, and never at any other. God is also sovereign in the places to which He sends revival and in the instruments He chooses to use. Looking back on the revival in Northampton and the surrounding district in 1735, Jonathan Edwards remarked:

> I think I have found that no discourses have been more remarkably blessed, than those in which the doctrine of God's absolute sovereignty with regard to the salvation of sinners, and his just liberty with regard to answering the prayers, or succeeding [prospering] the pains of natural man, continuing such, have been insisted upon.[2]

---

1. See Ernest Baker, *The Revivals of the Bible* (London: Kingsgate Press, 1906).
2. Edwards, *Faithful Narrative of Surprising Conversions*, 1:353.

The kind of men God used were characterized by earnestness in their work, who "ploughed and sowed in hope"; these were men who labored in patience, believing they would reap if they fainted not. They were also preeminently men of prayer, who were "much alone with God, replenishing their own souls out of the living fountain that out of them might flow to their people rivers of living water."[3] Those ministers of the Establishment, who delivered their addresses on revival in 1840, likewise saw the crucial link between prayer and revival. Reverend Cumming of Dunbarney Parish, who assisted Burns in 1839, felt there was a connection between increased prayer and the coming crisis in the church: "And perhaps the recent effusion of the Holy Ghost dispensed to some favourable localities in Scotland may be partly owing to the spirit of earnest prayer awakened by the danger in which our establishment has been involved."[4]

## The Importance of Fellowship Meetings

It was not simply the ministers who prayed, however. The nineteenth-century evangelicals inherited in their parishes a tradition of fellowship meetings among their congregations dating back to the seventeenth century. These meetings varied slightly in format but normally consisted of prayer, reading of Scripture, and conversing about individual personal experience for mutual edification.[5] Evangelicals like McCheyne, therefore, fell heir to a "highly developed, indigenous tradition of home-based groups, and adapted its structured approach to corporate prayer as a key part of their own agenda for parish revitalisation."[6]

McCheyne was much in favor of such meetings, preferring a close meeting of four to five participants to an open one, as he expressed to

---

3. Andrew Bonar, as quoted in Gillies, *Historical Collections of Accounts of Revival*, vi–x.

4. *The Revival of Religion: Addresses by Scottish Evangelical Leaders Delivered in Glasgow in 1840* (Edinburgh: Banner of Truth Trust, 1984), 136.

5. *Presbyterian Review and Religious Journal*, April 1841: 106.

6. D. A. Currie, "The Growth of Evangelicalism in the Church of Scotland, 1793–1843" (PhD diss., St. Andrews University, 1991), 356.

a correspondent.[7] He advised meeting weekly at a convenient hour, being regular in attendance, and praying in secret before going.[8]

D. A. Currie has pointed out three values of fellowship meetings. First, the self-examination that was a part of the meeting may well have served to help awaken the people to their true spiritual condition. Second, the meetings helped to keep alive the content of what had been preached in the services and enabled those awakened earlier to reach the point of conversion. Third, as the revival died away, fellowship meetings and prayer groups served to keep up the interests of those who had been caught up in the awakening period.[9] If the thirty-nine prayer meetings that McCheyne found on his return in November 1839 had been following such advice, this, together with the fervent preaching and prayerful expectancy with which Andrew Bonar characterized their pastor, helps to explain why St. Peter's in particular was so blessed.[10] If every parish in the land that had prayer fellowships is taken into consideration, this could explain why McCheyne believed there was never a time when the Spirit of God was more present in Scotland.[11]

## The Contribution of Religious Periodicals

Another factor contributing to the awakening of a desire for revival was the evangelical emphasis of some of the leading religious periodicals. For example, the *Edinburgh Christian Instructor* made a plea, in 1832, for a "hortatory and affectionate style of preaching, abounding with appeals to the consciences, and invitations addressed to the hearts of sinners." This should take the place of the intellectual and

---

7. Andrew A. Bonar, *Memoir*, 275–76. McCheyne wrote in March 1840 to John Just: "One great rule in holding them is, that they be really meetings of disciples. If four or five of you that know the Lord would meet together regularly, you will find that far more profitable than a meeting open to all…. If a young man acquainted with any of you, becomes concerned about his soul, or a lively Christian is visiting any of you, these may be admitted; but do not make your meeting more open."

8. Andrew A. Bonar, *Memoir*, 276–77.

9. Currie, "Growth of Evangelicalism," 193.

10. Andrew A. Bonar, *Memoir*, 174.

11. Van Valen, *Constrained by His Love*, 337.

abstract style that prevailed.[12] The *Scottish Christian Herald*, which began publication in March 1836, was burdened to "carry religion home to the heart." McCheyne wrote an article for the *Herald* while at Larbert, defending unusual spiritual experiences associated with awakenings, such as "sudden conversions."[13] The *Presbyterian Review and Religious Journal* advocated special prayer for the outpouring of the Holy Spirit and defended revival vigorously when it came.[14]

The *Review* also took a stand against the views expressed by Finney in his *Lectures on Revival*, which appeared in Scotland in the late 1830s. Finney believed that revival was "a purely philosophical result of the right use of the constituted means."[15] In his thinking there was no imputation of Adam's sin, no transmitted corruption of the heart. God's part in religion and revival, according to Finney, was reduced to that of an "influence." Human beings are able to save themselves by the right use of their free will, there being no need for an inward work of the Holy Spirit.[16] The *Review* not only voiced a preference for the recently republished *Narrative of the Revival of Religion* by Jonathan Edwards but also gave its approval instead to the 1840 *Lectures on Revivals* by eminent American Presbyterian minister William B. Sprague. Sprague emphasized the sovereign agency of the Holy Spirit in revival: "The Spirit operates during a revival to bring into exercise a far more vigorous and efficient human instrumentality than on ordinary occasions. He impresses more deeply with their responsibility, causing them to bring home the truth to the consciences of their hearers with unwonted earnestness."[17]

---

12. *Edinburgh Christian Instructor*, new series, 1, no. 7 (1832): 437–38, 446–48.

13. *Scottish Christian Herald*, May 28, 1836; Currie, "Growth of Evangelicalism," 114–15.

14. *Presbyterian Review and Religious Journal*, April 11, 1839: 64–69; Currie, "Growth of Evangelicalism," 102.

15. C. G. Finney, *Lectures on Revival of Religion* (London: Milner, 1838), 16, 21, 34, 235–50.

16. B. B. Warfield, *Perfectionism* (Grand Rapids: Baker, 1981), 2:173–79, 193. All God's influence in converting men, said Finney, is moral influence.

17. William B. Sprague, *Lectures on Revivals of Religion* (Edinburgh: Banner of Truth Trust, 1978), 110.

When Scottish evangelicals asked themselves, therefore, why they were not experiencing revival at home, their answer was that they should tread the old paths, give greater commitment to the traditional approach: increased prayer, regular weekly preaching of the gospel at the Sabbath services, looking all the time expectantly for the Holy Spirit to work. As the *Edinburgh Christian Instructor* put it: "We do not want new measures; but certainly we do desiderate a more vigorous and persevering employment of the old."[18] Burns and McCheyne were very much in agreement with this. Their approach differed very little from that of Whitefield and Robe at Cambuslang and Kilsyth a century earlier.

## Opposition to the Revival from within the Church

While the church is slumbering or holding its normal services without making any impact on a neighborhood, little attention is paid to it. When God sends revival and Christians are awakened and sinners converted in large numbers, however, the neighborhood sits up and takes note of events. Because of his uncompromising evangelical stance and his godly life, McCheyne was the object of much criticism. Bonar summarized how he was treated in his early years in this way:

> Yet during these pleasant days he had much reproach to bear. He was the object of supercilious contempt to formal, cold-hearted ministers, and bitter hatred to many of the ungodly. At this day there are both ministers and professing Christians of whom Jesus would say, "The world cannot hate you" (John 7:7), for the world cannot hate itself; but it was not so with Mr McCheyne. Very deep was the enmity borne to him by some—all the deeper, because the only cause of it was likeness to his Master. But nothing turned him aside.[19]

There was opposition also from within the ministry, particularly among the Moderates, that two such young men like Burns and McCheyne, not long entered upon the ministry, should have been so

---

18. *Edinburgh Christian Instructor*, 4th series, 2 (October 1839): 404–8.
19. Andrew A. Bonar, *Memoir*, 82–83.

used of God in these revival years and, by implication, not more seasoned ministers like themselves. Bonar had a ready answer for such, pointing out that God's sovereign grace shone out all the more:

> Do such objectors suppose that God ever intends the honour of man in a work of revival? Is it not the honour of His own name that He seeks? Had it been His wish to give the glory to man at all, then indeed it might have been asked, "Why does He pass by the older pastors, and call for the inexperienced youth?" But when sovereign grace was coming to bless a region in the way that would redound most to the glory of God, can we conceive a wiser plan than to use the sling of David in bringing down the Philistine?[20]

## Opposition from the Press

The press could at times be unsympathetic and even hostile to the work of revival. In a Fast Day sermon on Isaiah 22:12–14 in 1840, McCheyne let his feelings be known, without specifying any particular newspaper: "Is there a scheme of Popery to be set afoot? The Press will defend it. Is there a scheme of Christian philanthropy? The Press will besmear it with slanders. Is there a faithful servant of Christ, labouring night and day to win souls? The Newspaper will join with Satan in spitting on him, and do unspeakable harm."[21]

William Chalmers Burns came in for severe criticism in the press. The *Dundee Chronicle*, noted as an organ for radical politicians and support for voluntaryism in church government, launched a personal attack on Burns in October 1839, while the revival was still at its height. Burns was ridiculed as "a mere licentiate," the congregation as "a promiscuous rabble." The *Advertiser*, though not in favor of the

---

20. Andrew A. Bonar, *Memoir*, 122. He reinforced this point by referring to the words of Baxter in his *Reformed Pastor*, who remonstrated with the jealous ministers of his day: "What! Malign Christ in gifts for which he should have the glory, and all because they seem to hinder our glory! Does not every man owe thanks to God for his brethren's gifts, not only as having himself part in them…but also because his own ends may be attained by his brethren's gifts as well as his own?"

21. McCheyne, *Passionate Preacher*, 48.

Established Church, nevertheless came to Burns's defense, suggesting the writer of the article was stirred against the minister because of his "indefatigable industry": "This is a quality, however, too valuable and too rare, not to be much prized by the people. We do like to see it, even when we do not altogether approve of the direction it takes; and, in the case of Mr Burns, we have met with none who deny his sincerity, or refuse him the credit of devotedness to the cause which he believes to be a good one."[22]

Another local correspondent, calling himself Laicus, came to the defense of what was happening at St. Peter's in those months. Objection had been raised to three things: undue excitement, late hours, and irreverence. To the first he replied that no objection was ever raised when there was excitement over politics, music, dancing, or theater, not to mention Chartist speeches and trade union meetings. Second, he asked why there were complaints about females coming home late from church meetings when wives, sisters, and daughters could stay up till 5 or 6 a.m. at balls. As to irreverence, Laicus commented, "I have had every opportunity of judging, but could never discover any irreverence in what Mr Burns or those who assisted him have said or done."[23]

Even after the revival was past its peak, some elements of the press pursued Burns. After being used in revival in St. Leonard's Church in Perth for some months, he left for Aberdeen in the spring of 1840, after repeated requests to come and preach there. He spent several months there, preaching in Bonaccord Church, the North Church, and very often to crowds in the open air in venues like Castle Street.[24] At the beginning of January 1841, an article appeared in the *London Times* that was carried in the *Edinburgh Courant* and was printed locally in the *Dundee Advertiser*. It was the work of a reporter for the *Aberdeen Herald*, who had observed only one meeting for inquir-

---

22. *Dundee, Perth, and Cupar Advertiser*, Friday, October 26, 1839. The *Chronicle* issue for October of that year is, unfortunately, not extant.

23. *Dundee, Perth, and Cupar Advertiser*, Friday, October 26, 1839.

24. McMullen, *God's Polished Arrow*, 50–51; Islay Burns, *Memoir*, 158–65.

ers in Bonaccord Church on November 23, 1840. He launched into a scathing attack on Burns:

> A clerical stripling in particular, having neither realized his professed intention of labouring in the Heathen lands, nor been so fortunate as to obtain a benefice at home, has long been endeavouring to attract the notice of pious patrons and vacant parishes, by a succession of the most profane and revolting extravagances that were ever heard of, under pretext of awakening and converting people. From his native parish of Kilsyth...the youthful Revivalist, still remaining unbeneficed, went over to try his chance at Dundee. There, as in his own town, his spiritual *Mesmerism* is said to have affected miracles of grace.... The Holy Spirit, no longer diffusing His blessed influences irrespective of private favouritism, was represented as being more accessible to this beardless apostle than to all his quiet and venerable seniors put together.

The *Advertiser* subjoined to this report comments from Reverend Parker of Aberdeen, one of the revival party. His on-the-spot observations were quite different. He saw some tears, heard a good deal of sighing and sobbing, and could wish for more of it, considering the hard-hearted people he had to deal with. Burns seemed to be able to reach the hearts of the people, and the Spirit was with him.[25] Because this was happening within the "bounds" of Aberdeen Presbytery, a committee of that body compiled a series of fifteen questions to determine the nature of the revival work in that area. Similar questions were sent to other parts of the country where revivals had recently occurred or were still taking place.[26]

---

25. *Dundee, Perth, and Cupar Advertiser*, Friday, January 1, 1841.

26. See Gillies, *Historical Collections of Accounts of Revival*, 558–60, for the answers given to some of the fifteen questions by Andrew Gray of Perth, John Milne of Perth, Alexander Cumming of Dunbarney, Horatius Bonar of Kelso, Andrew Bonar of Collace, Robert MacDonald of Blairgowrie, John Purves of Jedburgh, and Dugald Campbell of Breadalbane. Horatius Bonar, *Life of the Rev. John Milne*, 48–65.

## McCheyne's Impartial Assessment of the Dundee Revival

McCheyne received his copy of the fifteen questions and responded by March 1841 (see appendix 2 for the list of fifteen questions). It is clear he was not in the least cowed or intimidated by the questions put but answered frankly and as fairly and fully as he could, giving a balanced account. Some of the questions he grouped together to answer. The first question asked whether revival had taken place in his parish or district, to what extent, by what instrumentality, and by what means. A full fifteen months since his return from Palestine, McCheyne had ample time to acquaint himself with the situation. He began by describing what had taken place as "a very remarkable and glorious work of God, in the conversion of sinners and edifying of saints." This was something that dated from his arrival in November 1836 and continued up to the present, but "was much more remarkable in the autumn of 1839." The means used, McCheyne wrote, were of the ordinary kind. Here he detailed the normal meetings, which have been outlined in chapter 3. It was "immediately after the beginning of the Lord's work at Kilsyth," when "the word of God came with such power to the hearts and consciences of the people." Such was the thirst that for nearly four months "it was found desirable to have public worship almost every night." He referred to the thirty-nine prayer meetings he found on his return from Palestine. Most of these meetings were still in progress. McCheyne acknowledged the several ministers who had given assistance at the height of the revival. As to the extent of the work, people from all quarters of the town had been affected, "belonging to all ranks and denominations of the people." He refrained from giving an exact number of converted, but mentioned many hundreds who had come to be counseled by the ministers. He ended this question with these words: "so that I am deeply persuaded, the number of those who have received saving benefit is greater than any one will know till the judgment day."

Questions 2 and 3 he took together. They asked about the previous life of individuals, how their lives had changed, and how they attended to the means of grace. The converts came from various backgrounds, "not a few in the higher ranks of life that seem evidently to have become new creatures, who previously lived a worldly life, though unmarked by open wickedness." Many who had been nominal churchgoers had also found the Savior. Again, many who had descended into the depths of sin had been wonderfully saved.

When asked in question 4 to give a number for those who had been saved, he referred to six to seven hundred who had been counseled by ministers in the autumn of 1839. He was aware, however, that there were many more concerned about their souls who never approached anyone. At the time of writing his replies, he was hearing of new cases of inquirers.

Question 5 asked about the conduct of those who had professed salvation. McCheyne answered honestly. He was clear that "it pleased God at that time to bring an awfully solemn sense of divine things over the minds of men. It was, indeed, the day of our merciful visitation." Many who had at that time expressed concern about their sins, however, had gone back into the world. On the other hand, there were those who had "walked consistently for four years," though some had their falls, and others had left their first love. McCheyne cited as evidence of increased spiritual life that the people themselves had asked for an additional Communion on his return. This was held in January 1840 (the previous one being in October 1839), "the happiest and holiest that I was ever present at." During that Communion a thank offering was uplifted on the Monday. Even though these were hard times in Dundee, 71 pounds was collected for missionary work.

Question 6 asked about beneficial effects on the religious condition of the people at large. McCheyne had one negative point to make—that multitudes "of those who live within the sound of the Sabbath bell continue to live on in sin and misery." There were, however, four positive effects from the awakening. First, "many from a distance have become heirs of glory." Second, such an impact had been made that even the ungodly were prepared to grant that there was such a thing as conversion. There was, third, a greater observance of and reverence for the Sabbath and the house of God. Last, the prayer meetings had made a tremendous impact, spreading "a sweet influence over the place." Visiting ministers would be quick to discern "that there are many praying people in the congregation."

Questions 7 to 9 concerned that which some found objectionable about times of revival—the "phenomena," or "excesses," as some would call them. McCheyne took all three together. He began by referring to St. Peter's as a "Bochim," a place of weepers, something he had desired and prayed for even before his departure for Palestine. Since his return he saw some people who could not restrain their feelings, sighs from many a heart, and individuals crying aloud. This had been witnessed by the different ministers who had assisted at the revival and Communion times. These expressions from members of the congregation often "occurred under the most tender gospel invitations." Some cried out in deepest agony. This was actually blessed by God to awaken careless sinners who had come merely to mock. Far from being on the defensive here, McCheyne ended his answer to this question by saying that they ought to be praying for such solemn times, that "our slumbering congregations shall be made to cry out, 'Men and brethren, what shall we do?'"

In questions 10 and 11 he was asked how long the revival meetings lasted and whether he approved or disapproved of such meetings on the whole. McCheyne began his answer by asserting that none of the ministers involved in the work in Dundee had ever used the term "revival meeting," nor did they approve of its use. He then pointed to the Acts of the Apostles, where they preached and taught the gospel daily. Yet never were their meetings called revival meetings. In St. Peter's, meetings were held for preaching and teaching of the gospel and for prayer. No other services took place. With regard to the length of meetings, during the autumn of 1839, meetings normally ended at ten o'clock p.m. Sometimes out of necessity they were prolonged for counsel and prayer. McCheyne could recall a few occasions when the services went on until midnight. This was because after the benediction had been pronounced, the majority of the people remained in their seats or in the passages. They were spoken to again, then "singing and prayer filled up the rest of the time." He commented on this: "On such occasions I have often longed that all the ministers in Scotland were present, that they might learn more deeply what the true end of our ministry is." His experience was that nothing indecorous took place on those occasions. He concluded his answer to these two questions with these words: "I do entirely and solemnly approve of such meetings, because I believe them to be in accordance with the word of God, to be pervaded by the Spirit of Christ, and to be ofttimes the birthplace of precious, never-dying souls. It is my earnest prayer that we may yet see greater things than these in all parts of Scotland."

Question 12 asked whether there had been any deaths due to overexcitement. McCheyne mentioned one case that enemies of the cause attributed to the meetings. The facts, however, when revealed, "clearly show that this was a groundless calumny."

Question 13 asked McCheyne to supply any additional information about the revival that could further illuminate the subject. Here he compared what had taken place in Dundee with what he knew of earlier revivals at Shotts, Cambuslang, Kilsyth, and in New England. The objections to revival in his day were the same as those raised in earlier centuries. These objections had been admirably answered by James Robe in his *Narrative* and Jonathan Edwards in his *Thoughts on the Revival of Religion in New England*.

Still probing in their penultimate question, the committee asked if there was anything peculiar in the preaching or "ministrations of the instruments." They were looking for something out of the ordinary. McCheyne responded by stating that there was nothing peculiar or different from what ought to characterize true ministers of Christ. They had preached the pure gospel of the grace of God. None of them read their sermons. He then characterized their preaching as follows:

They all, I think, seek the immediate conversion of the people, and they believe that, under a living Gospel ministry, success is more or less the rule, and want of success the exception. They are, I believe, in general, peculiarly given to secret prayer; and they have also been accustomed to have much united prayer when together, and especially before and after engaging in public worship. Some of them have been peculiarly aided in declaring the terrors of the Lord, and others in setting forth the fullness and freeness of Christ as the Savior of sinners; and the same persons have been, at different times, remarkably assisted in both these ways. So far as I am aware, no unscriptural doctrines have been taught, nor has there been a keeping back of any part of "the whole counsel of God."[27]

In this way did McCheyne describe those ministerial colleagues who labored faithfully with him in the gospel.[28]

When the replies from the various centers of revival were collated, "the result was a remarkable concurrence of weighty and impressive testimony alike to the depth and extent of the holy and enduring fruit in the hearts and lives of multitudes of its subjects."[29] The Aberdeen Presbytery's committee summed up the general results of their investigation in favorable terms:

> That a revival of religion, consisting in the general awakening of believers, and the conversion of multitudes of unbelievers, by the Holy Spirit, cannot but be an object of most earnest desire to every follower of the Lord.... That the evidence derived from answers to certain queries sent by the Committee of ministers and others in different parts of the country, amply bears out the fact that an extensive and delightful work of revival has commenced, and is in hopeful progress in various districts of Scotland—the origin of which, instrumentally, is to be traced to a more widely diffused spirit of prayer on the parts of ministers and people, and to the simple, earnest, and affectionate preaching of the gospel of the grace of God.[30]

Six months after submitting his answers to the Aberdeen Presbytery's questions, on October 5, 1841, McCheyne wrote to the convenor of the Synod of Merse and Teviotdale, with the revivals at Dundee and Perth, in particular, in mind: "I do not think I can lay any more facts

---

27. Andrew A. Bonar, *Memoir*, 544–51.
28. See chapter 6 for a discussion of the last question regarding children.
29. Islay Burns, *Memoir*, 185.
30. Islay Burns, *Memoir*, 185.

before your committee than those contained in the Aberdeen letter. Only this I would say, that half is not told you; no words can describe the scenes that have taken place in this place, when God the Spirit moved on the face of our assemblies. The glory is greatly departed; but the number of saved souls is far beyond my knowledge."[31]

---

31. As quoted in Horatius Bonar, *Life of the Rev. John Milne*, 65.

# 8

# Aftermath

The converts in these places [Kilsyth and Dundee] are Christians of a superior style to the professors who have long filled the Church.... They have exemplified nobly the rare virtue of making sacrifice for the sake of Christ, and the consequence of having identified themselves so completely with him is that they are joyful and assured believers. They know whom they have believed.
—James Hamilton to a relative in England

I suppose the worst time in the Christian church is generally that which follows the excitement of a revival; and if that revival has had no reality in it, the mischief which is done is awful and incalculable. If no excitement shall come at all, the mischief is still as great; God's people, being disappointed, have little heart to listen to further exhortations to future zealous action, become contented with their Laodicean lukewarmness, and it becomes impossible to bestir them again.
—C. H. Spurgeon, "Preparation for Revival,"
a sermon on Amos 3:3

James Hamilton was a close friend of McCheyne and the Bonars. From firsthand acquaintance he could testify to the efficacy of the believing prayers of pastor and people. Nowhere, he maintained, did he feel the reality of true Christian religion "more irresistibly" than in Dundee. It is not surprising, therefore, that a fire was kindled that spread out from Dundee into the countryside around.[1] Indeed, when the work of revival at Kilsyth and Dundee became known throughout the land, "the idea of revival as the great necessity of the Church and of the age...took strong possession of the minds of Christian men."[2]

## Burns Defends the Revival in Dundee

While still involved in revival in Perth, along with Reverend John Milne and others, William Burns defended the reality of the work that had taken place in Dundee the previous year. Preaching in St. Leonard's Church on March 11, 1840, on Ezekiel 37, "The Valley of Vision," he said, regarding verse 7:

> The prophet obeyed the command of Jehovah, hopeless as his endeavours might have appeared to him, and, lo! a shaking among the dry bones. Sinners first begin to be concerned, then anxious about their state, and then alarmed, and that some-times so greatly, that it cannot be concealed in their outward deportment. Sleep flies from them, and tears are their portion night and day. But is this not very natural? And yet, when it is so, it is often called enthusiasm and madness. In Dundee lately, something of this kind was witnessed, and it was therefore denounced as not being the true work of God, because some cried out and wept bitterly, groaning as they felt themselves under the dominion of Satan, and got a sight of sin in their own hearts. It was on that occasion said by a well-known and very godly Minister, from the north of Scotland,[3] who visited Dundee in order to assure himself whether it were, indeed, the Spirit of God who was working there, "when bone comes to bone, will there be no shaking heard?" And what time is more likely for such feelings as this, as when numbers of sinners are at once and together convinced of sin. Ah! will there be no extraordinary feelings, no excitement more than usual, when men first awake from the sleep of death, when they first see that hell from which they are escaping, and whose iron gates

---

1. Philip, *Evangel in Gowrie*, 308.
2. Yeaworth, "Robert Murray McCheyne," 320.
3. Dr. John MacDonald of Ferintosh.

are newly barred behind them?... A man *must* feel at such a time; it is impossible but that he should feel, and that with a depth unknown to him before.[4]

In this way did Burns give his own answer to questions 7 to 9 of the Aberdeen Presbytery's committee. What he and others had witnessed was strong indication of a deep work of conviction by the Spirit of God in the hearts of many of those who sat under the preaching in those months in 1839.

## Limitations to the Revival in Dundee

There were, however, some limitations to the extent of the revival in Dundee, at least in its initial stages. The opposition within Dundee, from Moderates and others, has already been noted. There was a small nucleus of evangelical ministers who did support the revival. The presence of others from a distance, however, such as Cumming of Dunbarney, Grierson of Errol, Bonar of Collace, and MacDonald of Blairgowrie, not to mention some from farther afield, gives substance to the comment of one of McCheyne's correspondents, Agnes Crow, who, with her friends, wrote to him on his return from Palestine to say that few of the Dundee ministers had assisted in the work at St. Peter's.[5] Second, although there were thirty-nine prayer meetings at the height of the revival, these were only over part of the town. Reverend William Borwick, writing a generation later, contrasted the situation in 1839 with the revival of 1859–1860. In the latter, revival prayer meetings were found all over the town.[6] Third, while many of the workers in the mills seem to have been blessed in the awakening, the rich who lived at a distance from St. Peter's and commuted in were largely untouched. McCheyne wrote to Burns on December 2,

---

4. William C. Burns, *Revival Sermons: Notes of Addresses*, ed. M. F. Barbour (Edinburgh: Banner of Truth Trust, 1980), 160–61.

5. Agnes Crow and others to McCheyne, November 30, 1839, MACCH 2.5.1.

6. William Reid, *Authentic Records of Revival Now in Progress in the United Kingdom* (Wheaton, Ill.: R. O. Roberts, 1980), 178; Lennie, *Land of Many Revivals*, 333.

1839: "The people were much alive in the Lord's service. But oh, dear brother, the most are Christless still! The rich are almost untroubled."[7]

## The Free Church Established in the Dundee Area

McCheyne was called home two months before the godly exodus of May 18, 1843, which led to the formation of the Free Church. He had, for the most part, carried his managers, elders, and congregation with him in his outspoken championship of Non-Intrusion and the spiritual independence of the church. Those of like mind with him lost no time. On May 18, twenty-four ministers and elders of Dundee Presbytery signed a protest of withdrawal from the Establishment they had loved and prized, because of "interference with conscience, the dishonour done to Christ's crown, and the rejection of His sole and supreme authority as King in His Church."[8] The kirk session minutes of St. David's Parish put it more bluntly. It had become very plain that they must leave the Establishment to enjoy freedom from civil control. If they remained in they would be "involved in the guilt of turning Christ's Household into Caesar's Household and putting the Crown of Christ on the Head of the Civil Magistrate."[9] The Act of Separation and Deed of Demission was executed on May 23. While they renounced their connection with the Establishment as ministers and elders, they in no way surrendered their rights as ministers of Christ's gospel. They would continue to perform their functions to as many members of their congregations as would adhere to them.[10] Almost the entire congregation of St. Peter's, 993 members and 14 elders, "came out."[11] By July 1843 there were eight town and six county congregations "within the bounds," adhering to the Free Church. This increased gradually to nineteen and then twenty by

---

7. Andrew A. Bonar, *Memoir*, 120.

8. Free Church Presbytery Minutes, May 18, 1843–1849, Dundee City Archives, MS CH3/19/3.

9. Kirk-Session Records of St. David's Parish Church, May 8, 1843. In June they separated from the Establishment.

10. Free Church Presbytery Minutes, May 23, 1843.

11. Robertson, *Awakening*, 183.

1848.[12] There was, therefore, quite a large exodus in the Dundee area. The Free Church also had a controlling interest on the town council for a time.[13] There were now in Dundee three main Presbyterian bodies: the Established Churches, the voluntary churches, and now the Free Church congregations.

## Successors to McCheyne

As an interim measure, Alexander Gatherer continued for a few months as caretaker pastor and missionary at St. Peter's. In May, however, the Free Church Presbytery decided to proceed with the ordination and admission of Islay Burns, younger brother of William Chalmers Burns. His ordination took place in June.[14] A godly man, Islay Burns was replacing one greatly beloved of his congregation, a tireless worker, and a magnetic personality. It is recorded that he sought, to begin with, to follow the preaching style of McCheyne, who had excelled both as teacher and evangelist. Realizing, however, that he had his own gift, he settled for a concentration on the teaching of Scripture, with responsibility also for preaching the gospel. Burns was to remain there until 1864, when he removed to Glasgow to become principal of the Free Church College. Following McCheyne's death, the number of people attending St. Peter's declined somewhat. Some moved to other parishes in Dundee, though the vast majority remained where they had been so blessed.[15]

## Coping with Declension

The church records in the years immediately after the revival reveal a gradually changing picture of a church still striving to fulfill its commission as before, but faced with quite an uphill task in a gradually changing spiritual climate. Many were admitted to membership who

---

12. Free Church Presbytery Minutes, July 9, 1845; April 19, 1848.

13. Drummond and Bulloch, *Church in Victorian Scotland*, 124.

14. Free Church Presbytery Minutes, April 5 and May 3, 1843. He was the first minister to be inducted in the new Free Church.

15. Van Valen, *Constrained by His Love*, 453–54; Lennie, *Land of Many Revivals*, 453n43.

had been converted in the revival years. Three times in 1843, communicants within the bounds of other parishes were received into fellowship.[16] The following year, over one thousand communicants were on the roll: "Of these upwards of 600 are parochial and 400 extraparochial." This would indicate something of the citywide influence of the revival and of McCheyne's appeal. Four elders and four deacons were to have oversight of the extraparochial, and the remaining eighteen elders and deacons were to have responsibility for 617 parochial communicants.[17]

Strenuous attempts were made to continue with the strong pastoral care that had characterized the McCheyne years. At the first meeting of the new kirk session in October 1843, it was resolved unanimously that elders would "continue to superintend the districts formerly assigned to them, in so far as the communicants adhering to the Free Church are concerned."[18] The following March, elders and deacons were instructed to visit the flock pastorally to find out their spiritual state. Each elder was to have the oversight of no more than fifty people.[19] A committee was set up to oversee the two schools at St. Peter's and also the Sabbath schools.[20] Five years later, instructions were given for teaching children of members of the congregation. Four elders were to supervise and be involved in catechizing the children, using the Bible and Shorter Catechism, beginning and ending with devotional exercises. Obviously they were trying to hold on to the young, who, they hoped, would be future church members.[21]

The records soon begin to reveal, however, cause for concern. Early in 1845 the kirk session had "cause to mourn over the declension of many who at one time gave tokens of spiritual life—and over the prevalence of Sabbath profanation, particularly among the

---

16. St. Peter's Free Church Kirk-Session Minutes, June 30, November 29, and December 6, 1843, Dundee City Archives, MS CH3/338/1.

17. St. Peter's Free Church Kirk-Session Minutes, March 4, 1844.

18. St. Peter's Free Church Kirk-Session Minutes, October 28, 1843.

19. St. Peter's Free Church Kirk-Session Minutes, March 1844.

20. St. Peter's Free Church Kirk-Session Minutes, October 28, 1843; March 14, 1845; and May 6, 1846.

21. St. Peter's Free Church Kirk-Session Minutes, December 1849.

young."[22] What they called for was increased energy, increased faithfulness, and increased prayer. One feature—indeed, one strength—of the McCheyne years had been the prayers of the Lord's people. After their pastor's death, some people had begun an eight-day concert for prayer, "in order to humiliation before the Lord."[23] That this did not last was made plain when William Middleton, printer, always ready to give the Dundee reading public an update on religious affairs, published Islay Burns's sermon "The Church's Hope and the Church's Danger," delivered on May 10, 1846. In it Burns made reference to many forsaking attendance at prayer meetings. He detected a spirit of complaining among the people rather than of praying, "of carnal regrets than godly sorrow and earnestly seeking after God…. We must arise and seek the Lord with all our heart if we would indeed find him." Burns pointed to the crucial role of those who were on the mount praying "while we were on the battlefield fighting." He dreaded the congregation turning into a soul-withering "lifeless orthodoxy."[24]

The presbytery records expressed great concern from 1844 on about the many pouring into Dundee and going to no place of worship. The population of the west end of Dundee had been growing rapidly. Earlier, it was noted that at the time of the church extension committee's recommendation of two new parishes for Dundee, that St. John's and St. Peter's could have done with a further parish created in their area.[25] McCheyne noted in his answers to the Aberdeen Presbytery that Dundee was a town of sixty thousand souls.[26] By 1851, the census figure was seventy-nine thousand.[27] A phrase found in the records from 1844 on is the "outfield population," with particular reference to

---

22. St. Peter's Free Church Kirk-Session Minutes, January 15, 1845.

23. Andrew A. Bonar, *Diary and Letters*, 106.

24. Islay Burns, *The Church's Hope and the Church's Dangers…* (Dundee, Scotland: William Middleton, 1846).

25. *Report of the Presbyterial Committee on Church Extension* (Dundee, Scotland: Chronicle Office, 1839), 3–4, 7.

26. Andrew A. Bonar, *Memoir*, 545.

27. Lythe and Butt, *Economic History of Scotland*, 245 (appendix 2, "Population of the Principle Towns"). The population rose to ninety thousand in 1861.

Dundee.[28] The presbytery felt bound to reclaim "that large and rapidly expanding territory which lies wild and waste." The minutes refer to thousands growing up in ignorance and crime. Thousands were living beside places of worship that they had no connection with. There were problems also within, with the "creeping in of false and erroneous doctrines, the prevalence of intemperance and Sabbath profanation."[29] Later that same month the presbytery recorded "an apparent deadness and indifference in the great body of the Congregations," young men no longer availing themselves of classes for instruction. Moreover, weekday prayer meetings were poorly attended.[30] By mid-century it was still the "outfield population" that the presbytery was making strenuous efforts to reach, those who "are at present estranged from the ordinances and the means of grace."[31]

The demographic shift referred to at the start of chapter 1 is one of the greatest—if not *the* greatest—challenges that the church has had to face in modern times (apart from the enemy within in terms of higher criticism and worldliness). It was a nationwide problem that the church extension programs alone could not solve. Thomas Chalmers, leader of the Free Church until his death in 1847, emphasized the missionary necessity of his church with these words (speaking of the Glasgow area): "Don't think that it is necessary that you should travel thousands of miles, or that you have immense oceans to traverse, before you can engage in a missionary work. There are wretched creatures in many parts of this town who are at as great a moral distance from the gospel, and from all its lessons, as if they had been born and lived all their days in the wilds of Tartary."[32]

---

28. There was sought at presbytery meetings the "best mode of making an aggressive movement on the outfield population within the bounds, and especially in the town of Dundee." Free Church Presbytery Minutes, July 3, July 10, and August 7, 1844; April 2, 1845.

29. Free Church Presbytery Minutes, September 12, 1849.

30. Free Church Presbytery Minutes, September 27, 1849.

31. Free Church Presbytery Minutes, December 12, 1848; St. Peter's Free Church Kirk-Session Minutes, January 22, 1850.

32. Thomas Chalmers, *Churches and Schools for the Working Classes* (Edinburgh: John Lowe, 1846), 6.

## Burns and McCheyne: Blessings That Endured

The ministry of Burns and McCheyne in Dundee was character-ized by deep self-abasement and complete reliance on God for daily strength for service. This found expression, as has been shown, in an ever-growing prayer life,[33] as they devoted themselves tirelessly to the work to which they had undoubtedly been called. They did so out of a great love for their Master. In an article reviewing Bonar's *Memoir* in 1844, one person wrote of McCheyne that "it might truly be said, 'the love of Christ constrained him.' He had pressed into a holy intimacy with his ascended Savior, and had surrendered his soul to the fervour of an unreserved affection, and made no secret of it: 'for me to live is Christ.'"[34]

There remain two questions: first, how best to explain why Burns and McCheyne were so used and honored of God. The second is, In spite of the obvious declension following the revival, what evidence is there of lasting influence from the Burns and McCheyne years?

Foremost among the reasons in answer to the first question was the importance of being convinced they were in the place God wanted them to be. McCheyne had been in St. Peter's only a few months—in fact, he was hardly settled—when in January 1837 came the first of several attempts to attract him to other charges. Skirling was a small rural parish on the western edge of Peebleshire, two and a half miles from Biggar. This parish had at least five attractions. There were only three hundred people in the parish. The country air would have been good for his poor health. He was offered twice the emolument he would get in Dundee. There would be time for him to pursue more studies on his own and perhaps develop his literary gifts. It would also have enabled him to pursue rural activities, for example the horse rid-ing of which he was so fond. Altogether quite a tempting offer!

In his reply to Lady Carmichael, who had exerted her influence to procure his services, McCheyne had no difficulty in declining:

---

33. McCheyne believed one of the reasons he was laid aside was to deepen his prayer life. Andrew A. Bonar, *Memoir*, 22, 85, 222.

34. *Presbyterian Review and Religious Journal* 65 (July 1844): 231. Reviewer unknown.

Still, Dear Madam, I am here, I did not bring myself here. I did not ask to be made a candidate for this place. I was hardly willing to be a candidate.... I was as happy at Larbert as the day was long.... And yet God has turned the hearts of this whole people towards me like the heart of one man.... To be where He would have us be…that is heaven upon earth, wherever our home may be, in a cottage, or in a castle, or with John in a dungeon.[35]

The following month he received a call to St. Leonard's, Perth. He also turned this down: "I feel more and more happy in Dundee, so that I shall be quite happy to remain if I see clearly that I should."[36] St. Martin's Parish, near Perth, was also turned down. What reinforced his decision was an answer to prayer: some of his flock were awakened with concern for their souls.[37] To a correspondent he wrote at that time: "Ever since I was asked to go to St M. souls have been brought from darkness to light—born again under my ministry."[38]

Late in 1841, McCheyne received a call to Kettle in Fife. Again his reply indicated his resolve to remain: "I *dare not*, and *could not*.... I have never wanted success. I do not think I can speak a month in this parish without winning some souls." He was now the spiritual father to hundreds. Considering his stern language about false shepherds, how could he desert them, "when the clouds of adversity are beginning to lower."[39] In Dundee, therefore, McCheyne stayed for the rest of his short ministry.

---

35. McCheyne to Lady Carmichael, January 20, 1837, MACCH 2.1.6. Three days later he wrote to his father, acknowledging the benefits of a parish like Skirling, saying: "I dare not leave this people.... God has set me down among the noisy mechanics and political weavers of this godless town.... He will make me a practical Divine at least which is the best of all Divinity in guiding souls to heaven.... I am quite sure it is the will of God that I should remain here." McCheyne to Papa, January 23, 1837, MACCH 2.1.7.

36. McCheyne to Papa, February 3, 1837, MACCH 2.1.9.

37. Andrew A. Bonar, *Memoir*, 67–68.

38. McCheyne to J. M. Nairne, September 4, 1837, MACCH 2.1.20.

39. Andrew A. Bonar, *Memoir*, 139–40; Smellie, *Robert Murray McCheyne*, 122; and Van Valen, *Constrained by His Love*, 389. The last phrase is a reference to the coming Disruption, which McCheyne believed was inevitable by this time.

In the case of Burns, the providence of God was at work, guiding events and circumstances to bring him to Dundee. While at Glasgow University, he had quite an exercise of soul to go as a missionary to India. Not getting a positive reply, he meantime applied to go to St. John's, New Brunswick, the colonial committee showing an interest. The India committee was not happy about this. Another possible avenue of service abroad for Burns was Ceylon. By March 2, 1839, however, Burns was writing to McCheyne to say he would like to make proof of his ministry at home before venturing abroad. He would count it an honor to watch over McCheyne's flock in his absence. Thus began his seven months at Dundee. Two months into his time there, the church's India committee asked Burns to go as a missionary to Poonah in Bombay. At the same time, the Jewish committee asked him to go to Aden in Arabia. By this time, however, he was committed to the work in St. Peter's. Service abroad had to wait another eight years, when he sailed to China to begin his life's work.[40]

Another important factor, well illustrated in particular from McCheyne's correspondence and sermons, was that these men were fully aware of the danger of a congregation being attracted to God's servant and bypassing Christ. Preaching from Isaiah 44:3–4 ("I will pour water"), he emphasized it is God who is the author in a work of grace; God who carries on the work, leading awakened persons to Christ. It is God who enlarges His people. The first lesson, then, was to look beyond ministers for a work of grace.[41] On another occasion, when news of his mission to the Jews became known, he wrote as follows to his flock from Edinburgh:

A minister will make a poor savior in the day of wrath. It is not knowing a minister, or loving one, or hearing one, or having a name to live, that will save. You need to have your hand on the head of the Lamb for yourselves (Lev. 1, 4). You need to have your eyes on the brazen serpent for yourselves (John iii, 14, 15).

---

40. Burns to McCheyne, March 2, 1839, MACCH 2.4.2; Islay Burns, *Memoir*, 56; and McMullen, *God's Polished Arrow*, 24.

41. McCheyne, *From the Preacher's Heart*, 82 (full text, 82–88). Preached in St. Peter's, July 1, 1838.

I fear I will need to be a swift witness against many of my people in the day of the Lord, that they looked to me, and not to Christ, when I preached to them.[42]

As he was about to depart for Palestine, he wrote to his friend Mrs. Thain: "This separation has been a most faithful chastisement. To those that liked the man but not the message—who were pleased with the vessel but not with the treasure—it will reveal the vanity of what they thought their good estate."[43] During his absence he kept in touch with his flock with his pastoral letters. In the first of these he referred to the sad error into which too many were falling, that of "leaning upon man," "mistaking friendship towards a minister for faith on the Son of God."[44]

McCheyne was always concerned lest there be false professions of faith. For that reason, as Bonar observed, he became "more vigilant and discriminating in dealing with souls"—so much so, that some felt there was a little coldness in his manner toward them. This detachment, however, was out of concern for their misplaced loyalties. His compassion for souls never wavered.[45] He constantly likened ministers to the pole in Numbers 21; it was to the brazen serpent they were to look.[46]

---

42. Andrew A. Bonar, *Memoir*, 88.

43. Andrew A. Bonar, *Memoir*, 213. From Edinburgh, March 15, 1839.

44. Andrew A. Bonar, *Memoir*, 219. In the same paragraph he wrote, "This time of trial is for your furtherance. Does not God teach you, by means of it, to look beyond man to the Savior, who abideth ever? Is not God showing you that ministers are earthen vessels, easily broken, and fit only to be cast aside like a broken pitcher out of mind? Is He not bidding you look more to the treasure which was in them, and which flows in all its fullness from Christ?"

45. Andrew A. Bonar, *Memoir*, 122–23.

46. Andrew A. Bonar, *Memoir*, 158–59. In his Thursday lectures on the seven churches of Asia, he said: "As I have told you before, the only use of the pole was to hold up the brazen serpent. No one thought of looking at the pole: so we are to hold up Christ in the sight of you all; we are to give testimony to the truth: we are witnesses for Christ, we are to hold up Jesus before you, and before ourselves too; so that we shall disappear, and nothing shall be seen but Christ." McCheyne, *Brief Expositions*, 6 (on Ephesus).

One of the striking features of McCheyne's ministry was the manner in which he addressed his hearers. There were no missing notes in his preaching. He preached a full gospel, calling the people constantly to repentance, speaking of hell and judgment, and insisting on the necessity of the saints persevering in the faith. This might have aroused opposition in some of his hearers. What remained with many of his listeners, however, was the way in which he addressed them. Bonar noted that at the various Communion seasons McCheyne spoke at, outside St. Peter's, "it was testified of him, that not the words he spoke, but the holy manner in which he spoke, was the chief means of arresting souls."[47] That this was a constant feature of his ministry can be seen by the comment made on the last public address he gave at Broughty Ferry on Isaiah 60:1, "Arise, shine; for thy light is come." A note was found on his desk unopened while he lay in the throes of typhus fever. The anonymous writer was obviously struck by the whole carriage of the preacher as he delivered his message:

> I heard you preach last Sabbath evening, and it pleased God to bless that sermon to my soul. It was not so much what you said, as your manner of speaking that struck me. I saw in you a beauty in holiness that I never saw before. You also said something in your prayer that struck me very much. It was "Thou knowest that we love Thee." Oh sir, what would I give that I could say to my blessed Savior, "Thou knowest that I love Thee!"[48]

McCheyne had a tender delivery of his message and was never unnecessarily abrasive.

That the manner in which truth is imparted, as well as the content of a message, can leave its mark is seen in the following incident recorded in the *Dundee Monthly Visitor* for November 1874. At a Bible class in a prison on a Sabbath evening, a certain woman was observed to become very thoughtful when Revelation 3 was read in her hearing. The next day she said to the reader that she had trembled on

---

47. Andrew A. Bonar, *Memoir*, 71.
48. Andrew A. Bonar, *Memoir*, 161–62.

hearing the passage read. When asked why, she said, "Oh, it was one of the chapters from which I once heard Mr McCheyne preach!" The article concluded with these words: "Reader, Mr McCheyne has now been thirty-one years with the Lord in glory, and see how his words were still bearing witness in the conscience of hearers who once had spurned them. In prison, this soul remembered its former Sabbaths and solemnities; in hell, it may be many souls will too late remember how often the Lord's messengers, and the Lord by their means, would have gathered them, and they would not."[49]

Burns and McCheyne were concerned not only that there should be no attraction to the man but that all done in those days should be supremely for God's glory. McCheyne was tested as to the reality of his concern for God's glory on his return from Palestine. He had written to Burns and prayed that he might be "a thousand times more blessed among them than ever I was."[50] He himself had labored tirelessly before going to Edinburgh. Now, on his return after the best part of a year, seeing the blessing that had come to the people in St. Peter's, what was his response? That first night back, after he had spoken to a packed St. Peter's, he said, "To Thy name, O Lord, to Thy name, O Lord, be all the glory!" Bonar wrote that McCheyne "had received from the Lord a holy disinterestedness that suppressed every feeling of envy." For himself McCheyne could claim he had no desire "but the salvation of my people, by whatever instrument."[51] McCheyne and Burns remained close friends and correspondents thereafter.

For Burns's part, what mattered more to him than anything else was the holiness and glory of God. What he feared above all else was "that any glory might go to him and not to the Lord."[52] How deeply

---

49. *Dundee Monthly Visitor*, November 1874, Dundee Local History Library, MS 174 (2c).

50. Andrew A. Bonar, *Memoir*, 88–89.

51. Andrew A. Bonar, *Memoir*, 116. Bonar noted also: "Although naturally ambitious, grace so wrought in him, that he never sought to bring himself into view; and most cheerfully would he observe and take notice of the grace and gifts of others." *Memoir*, 130.

52. McMullen, *God's Polished Arrow*, 9.

he felt the need for self-abasement is illustrated by a letter he wrote to McCheyne in January 1840 while he labored in Perth:

> I have been led to think that I will not be much blessed in the Lord's work again until he has abased me in His own sight, and taught me if not the people also to whom I preach in His holy name that I am indeed all vile, and that all the glory is His alone. Oh pray that this may not be shown by my fall but by my being chastened and humbled in the way that His infinite wisdom and love may choose.[53]

Burns's desire for the glory of God and of Christ was evident in his preaching. James Hamilton, then at Abernyte in Perthshire, observed him closely in the early weeks of revival in August 1839. What came through clearly was Burns's zeal for the glory of Christ more so than his desire for the salvation of sinners. Every motive was directed to the *exalting of Christ* in the gospel.[54]

As to the second question—What lasting influence was there from the Burns and McCheyne years?—consider first the immediate impact of McCheyne's death on his generation. The death of one of God's choice servants can often galvanize those who remain to greater efforts in His service. McCheyne himself felt for some time that the day when he would depart to be with Christ was fast approaching.[55] Nevertheless, his death left his family and friends grief stricken. James Hamilton, once at Abernyte in Perthshire but by this time minister at the Scots church in Regent Square, London, missed his friend deeply.[56] Andrew Bonar, McCheyne's closest friend, recorded in his diary, "Saturday 25th.... Never, never in all my life time have I felt anything like this. It is a blow to myself, to his people, to the Church of Christ in Scotland.... My heart is sore. It makes me feel death near myself now. Life has lost half its joys, were it not for the hope of

---

53. Burns to McCheyne, January 11, 1840, MACCH 2.4.6.

54. James Hamilton to J. Willis, August 27, 1839, in Arnot, *Life of James Hamilton*, 143.

55. Andrew A. Bonar, *Memoir*, 159.

56. Arnot, *Life of James Hamilton*, 212–14.

saving souls. There was no friend whom I loved like him."[57] For these two brethren the passing of McCheyne was a direct challenge to gird up their loins and aspire to greater efforts in the Lord's service. James Hamilton wrote to Bonar that the Lord was speaking in this providence, calling on ministers to "arise and begin anew.... I wish to hear His voice, and have been praying these days for a double portion of Elijah's spirit. Oh that the Lord would grant that double portion to many Elishas in Scotland also!"[58] To Bonar it was a challenge to live nearer to God, that McCheyne's mantle would fall on him: "Lord, grant me henceforth more holiness.... This terrible blow may be the answer to my prayers for holiness."[59] Twenty years later he wrote in his diary that the Lord made Robert McCheyne's death "a means of great blessing to me."[60]

Patrick Miller of Wallacetown Church in Dundee preached from the last verses of Romans 7 on the day after McCheyne's death. He spoke of him having been removed from them for two reasons: in mercy, in order to bring them closer to the Master, and in judgment "for prizing the man and forgetting the Master."[61] With this McCheyne would have agreed heartily. The Presbytery of Dundee (still at this point united and Established only) sought to present McCheyne's death as a challenge to all, that it might awaken the careless and backsliding and give the people of God a greater vision to rededicate themselves to His service.[62]

As to the lasting influence of the revival of those years, one clear evidence is the continuance of many in the spiritual pathway.

57. Andrew A. Bonar, *Diary and Letters*, 101.

58. Arnot, *Life of James Hamilton*, 214–15.

59. Andrew A. Bonar, *Diary and Letters*, 102–3.

60. Andrew A. Bonar, *Diary and Letters*, 235 (Sabbath, October 16, 1864).

61. Andrew A. Bonar, *Diary and Letters*, 102.

62. MACCH 2.3.83, April 5, 1843, and minutes of the presbytery records for that date. The managers' minutes of St. Peter's Church (March 29, 1843) recorded their gratitude for the faithful labors of their late pastor, adding, "The meeting whilst they desire to bow in resignation under this afflictive dispensation would at the same time express their hope that it may be greatly blessed to themselves and the members of the congregation."

Many people, thirty years later, could point to the years 1839–1843 as the time of their conversion.[63] There was growth also in the immediate vicinity of St. Peter's. In spite of the evidence of declension in the church records, which would no doubt apply equally to the other church groups in the town, the attendance at St. Peter's increased. This may well have been in part because of the growing population in that area and the assiduous attempts, already outlined, to reach them. A mission outreach was begun in Taylor's Lane in 1855, on the opposite side of Perth Road from St. Peter's. This prospered, becoming eventually the McCheyne Memorial Church. It was opened by C. H. Spurgeon in 1870.[64]

One who was a lad at the time of the awakening, J. C. Smith, compiled a work in his old age in 1910. It is largely his reminiscences of those revival days. It has the value, however, of including extracts from several people, themselves well on in years by this time, who could look back on a work of grace wrought in their lives in the days of Burns and McCheyne. One eighty-four-year-old wrote to Smith of the abiding influence of McCheyne's ministry:

> I was only seventeen years of age then; today I am eighty-four, and his voice is as clear and sweet as ever, and his teaching has been profitable to me, has remained as the rule of my life all these long years. Often have I thanked the Lord, that brought me to Christ. Chosen not for good in me, in those days under such a holy man, for I have never heard preaching which had the same power over me since.[65]

One of the features of the revival, already noted, is the way quite a number of the congregation were under deep conviction of sin for some time before coming to faith in Christ. Smith wrote of a lady who had an awful time of conviction of sin in those days. She had never been under the sound of the gospel before, had never been challenged

---

63. Islay Burns, *Memoir*, x; Yeaworth, "Robert Murray McCheyne," 319.
64. Van Valen, *Constrained by His Love*, 455. It was at the crossroads of Hawkhill and Perth Roads.
65. Smith, *Robert Murray McCheyne*, 7.

about the needs of her soul. She was taken to meet McCheyne, who spoke to her while she wept copiously. After listening to his preaching in St. Peter's for some time, she at last found peace in believing in the Lord Jesus Christ.[66] One elderly person, by this time resident in Perthshire, recalled being "led into a widow's garret by the good Spirit of God." There some sisters were praying before going to St. Peter's. They took her to hear McCheyne preaching on John 4:10: "If thou knewest the gift of God…thou wouldest have asked of him." As she was greatly affected by the sermon, various Christian friends spoke to her in private. John Mathewson, one of the elders, spent some time counseling her. She told Smith, "I was born the second time in 1840, and now I am eighty-two years old."[67]

Mrs. Sime, referred to earlier in connection with reports given to McCheyne of prayer meetings, looked back over the decades. She was taken to St. Peter's the day it opened, when she was very young. She was among the young people who attended the church in great numbers, sitting at the foot of the pulpit stairs. For some time she was under conviction of sin by the Spirit and was often in the inquiry room for counsel. Then, finally, "the Holy Spirit of God drew me and showed me Jesus as the Savior of sinners, and blessed be His name, He has never left me from that day to this (say, 4th December 1906)."[68]

That the influence of the revival years could still be felt a generation later can be seen from John Macpherson's estimate in the late nineteenth century:

> I can scarcely look around me in this city of Dundee, or walk its streets, without seeing in living embodiment or other palpable form the genuine and well-tested fruits of that revival. Many of the converts of the Burns and McCheyne period are worthy office-bearers in the churches. Of the converts in St. Peter's alone, some sixteen became ministers of the gospel at home and abroad, some of whom are now the spiritual fathers of hundreds. In short, if we may judge men by their fruits, and

---

66. Smith, *Robert Murray McCheyne*, 25–26.
67. Smith, *Robert Murray McCheyne*, 33–34.
68. Smith, *Robert Murray McCheyne*, 131.

if the fruit of the Spirit ever appears in the lives of men, the revival of that period was a great work of the Holy Ghost.[69]

The work of 1839–1843 and subsequent movements of the Spirit prepared the way for the revival of 1859–1860, in which many of the converts of those earlier years would have been deeply involved.

---

69. MacPherson, *Revival and Revival Work*, 19–20.

# McCheyne's Involvement in the Religious Life of the Town

During his few years at St. Peter's, in addition to his preaching and regular systematic pastoral visitation, McCheyne always took a keen interest in the wider religious life of the town, his involvement being most impressive. While very much an Establishment figure, being recognized along with Roxburgh as a leader of the evangelicals,[1] he nevertheless welcomed preachers from other denominations into his pulpit. He also preached for others, such as the Methodists, and defended doing so in print.[2] There was, indeed, an ecumenical side to the revival. He gave his support to various causes in Dundee, such as the Seamen's Society; the Dundee Protestant Association, which he was instrumental in reviving; and the Dundee Juvenile Bible and Missionary Society. McCheyne was a great supporter of the Dundee Tract Society, which benefited from his literary skills. In one year close to two hundred thousand tracts were distributed in Dundee and neighboring towns.[3] His social conscience led him to take an interest in the Deaf and Dumb Institute and the work for the blind. He noted with approval the passage of Lord Shaftesbury's Mines Act of 1842, which banned the employment of females and boys less than ten years of age underground. His love for orphans led him to organize collections on

---

1. Yeaworth, "Robert Murray McCheyne," 23.

2. McCheyne to the editor of the *Dundee Warder*, July 6, 1842, titled "Communion with Brethren of Other Denominations," and printed in the *Warder*, Tuesday, July 12, 1842, in Andrew A. Bonar, *Memoir*, 605–12; Van Valen, *Constrained by His Love*, 374–76; and Lennie, *Land of Many Revivals*, 332.

3. Andrew A. Bonar, *Memoir*, 91; Robertson, *Awakening*, 184; and Yeaworth, "Robert Murray McCheyne," 181–82.

their behalf.[4] While at Larbert, he wrote an orphan hymn based on Hosea 14:3, "for in thee the fatherless findeth mercy," portraying God as father, mother, and friend of the orphans.[5] McCheyne was also convenor of Dundee Presbytery's Sabbath observance committee. In this capacity he wrote in 1841 to the shareholders of the Dundee and Arbroath Railway, opened a few years before, to protest their allowing the carrying of mail on the Sabbath.[6] This was followed at the end of that year by a letter to Lord Advocate M'Neill, quoting the fourth commandment and question 60 of the Shorter Catechism. At the same time, McCheyne put out a tract, "I Love the Lord's Day," giving reasons why the Lord's people should prize it and use it correctly.[7]

4. Yeaworth, "Robert Murray McCheyne," 179–80.
5. McCheyne to family, May 13, 1836, MACCH 2.6, 31.
6. *Dundee Warder*, June 1, 1841.
7. Andrew A. Bonar, *Memoir*, 594–605.

# Evidence on Revivals

Queries on the Subject of the Revival of Religion
in St. Peter's Parish, Dundee.

Submitted to a Committee of the Presbytery of Aberdeen.

I. Have revivals taken place in your parish or district; and, if so, to what extent, and by what instrumentality and means?

II. Do you know what was the previous character and habits of the parties?

III. Have any who are notorious for drunkenness, or other immoralities, neglect of family duties or public ordinances, abandoned their evil practices, and become remarkable for their diligence in the use of the means of grace?

IV. Could you condescend on the number of such cases?

V. Has the conduct of any of the parties been hitherto consistent; and how long has it lasted?

VI. Have the means to which the revivals are ascribed been attended with beneficial effects on the religious condition of the people at large?

VII. Were there public manifestations of physical excitement, as in audible sobs, groans, cries, screams, etc.?

VIII. Did any of the parties throw themselves into unusual postures?

IX. Were there any who fainted, fell into convulsions, or were ill in other respects?

X. How late have you ever known revival meetings last?

XI. Do you approve or disapprove of these meetings upon the whole? In either case, have the goodness to state why.

XII. Was any death occasioned, or said to be occasioned, by over-excitement in any such case? If so, state the circumstances, in so far as you know them.

XIII. State any other circumstances connected with revivals in your parish or district, which, though not involved in the foregoing queries, may tend to throw light upon the subject.


### Additional Queries.

XIV. What special circumstances in the preaching or ministrations of the instruments appear to have produced the results in each particular case which may have come under your notice?

XV. Did the person or persons whom you described as the instruments in producing the effects above adverted to address children? At what hour? In what special terms? And what might be the age of the youngest of them?[1]

---

1. Andrew A. Bonar, *Memoir*, 543–44.

# Bibliography

## Manuscripts and Collections

Constitution for St. Peter's Church, May 30, 1836. Dundee City Archives, Dundee, Scotland.

Dundee Presbytery Minutes, 1836–1847. Dundee City Archives, Dundee, Scotland.

Free Church Presbytery Minutes, 1843–1849. Dundee City Archives, Dundee, Scotland.

General Kirk-Session Minutes. Dundee City Archives, Dundee, Scotland.

Kirk-Session Records of St. David's Parish Church, 1834–1877. Dundee City Archives, Dundee, Scotland.

Managers' Minutes of St. Peter's Church, 1835–1843. Dundee City Archives, Dundee, Scotland.

Manuscript Notebooks and Letters of Robert Murray McCheyne. New College Library, Edinburgh University.

McCheyne, R. M. Sermon on Romans 10, verse 3. Dundee City Archives, Dundee, Scotland.

McGavin, James R. Speech delivered at the Anti-Church Endowment Meeting, held in Ward Chapel, Dundee, February 27, 1838. Lamb Collection 176(5), Local History Library, Dundee, Scotland.

Peter Carmichael Biographical Works. Dundee University Archive Room, Dundee, Scotland.

Robert Murray McCheyne to Alexander Smith, November 15, 1842 (letter). Dundee City Archives, Dundee, Scotland.

Robert Murray McCheyne to Miss Katherine Duncan, January 14, 1840 (letter). Dundee City Archives MS TD/87/1, Dundee, Scotland.

St. Peter's Free Church Kirk-Session Minutes, 1843–1855. Dundee City Archives, Dundee, Scotland.

**Primary Sources**

*Address on the operation of the Corn Laws; delivered at a public Meeting of the Inhabitants of Dundee, on Monday 11 May 1840.* Located in Local History Library, Dundee, Scotland.

*Annals of Dundee, being extracts from the* Dundee Advertiser, *1801–1840.* Compiled by A. C. Lamb and A. H. Millar. Dundee, Scotland, 1908.

Anti-Patronage meeting, Chartist outrage, assault upon St. Andrews' Church, April 2, 1841. Lamb Collection 17(10), Local History Library.

*Bagster's Bible.* Partly annotated by Robert Murray McCheyne. 2 vols. London: Samuel Bagster, 1828. Dundee City Archives.

Baxter, Richard. *The Reformed Pastor.* Edited by William Brown. London: Religious Tract Society, 1829.

Bonar, Andrew A. *Diary and Letters.* Edited by Marjory Bonar. London: Hodder & Stoughton, 1893.

———. *Memoir and Remains of the Rev. Robert Murray McCheyne.* New edition. Edinburgh: Oliphant, Anderson and Ferrier, 1892.

Bonar, Andrew A., and Robert Murray McCheyne. *Mission of Discovery: The Beginning of Modern Jewish Evangelism.* Edited by Allan M. Harman. Fearn, Scotland: Christian Focus, 1996.

Bonar, Horatius. *True Revivals and the Men God Uses.* London: Evangelical Press, n.d.

Buchanan, George. *Abstract of Report on the Proposed Plan for supplying the Town of Dundee with water.* Dundee, Scotland: D. Hill and Son, 1836.

Burns, Islay. *The Church's Hope and the Church's Dangers, with special reference to recent discussions, being the substance of a sermon preached in St. Peter's Church, Dundee, on Sabbath, 10th May, 1846*. Dundee, Scotland: William Middleton, 1846.

———. *Memoir of the Rev. William Chalmers Burns*. London: James Nisbet, 1870.

Burns, William C. *Revival Sermons: Notes of Addresses*. Edited by M. F. Barbour. Edinburgh: Banner of Truth Trust, 1980.

Carmichael, Peter. *The Dundee Textile Industry, 1790–1885: From the Papers of Peter Carmichael of Arthurstone*. Edited by Enid Gauldie. Scottish History Society, 4th series, vol. 6. Edinburgh: Constable for the Scottish Historical Society, 1969.

*Charters, Writs and Public Documents of the Royal Burgh of Dundee, the Hospital and Johnston's Bequest: 1292–1880*. Dundee, Scotland: D. R. Clark and Son, 1880.

*The Conversion of a Young Woman at St. Peter's, Dundee, in August 1839. Related by herself*. 3rd ed. Dundee, Scotland: William Middleton, 1841.

*Dundee in 1793 and 1833: The First and Second Statistical Accounts*. With an introduction by Annette M. Smith. Facsimile edition. St. Andrews: St. Andrews University Library, 1991.

*Dundee Monthly Visitor*, November 1874. Located at Dundee Local History Library.

Dick, William. *Remarks on Endemic Fever, Commonly Called Typhus*. Dundee, Scotland: Alexander Colville, 1820.

Edwards, Jonathan. "Some Letters Relating to the Revival." In *The Great Awakening*, ed. C. C. Goen, 533–66. Vol. 4 of *The Works of Jonathan Edwards*. New Haven, Conn.: Yale University Press, 1972.

———. *The Works of Jonathan Edwards*. Edited by Edward Hickman. 2 vols. Edinburgh: Banner of Truth Trust, 1976.

*Familiar Letters by the Rev. Robert Murray McCheyne*. Edited by [Adam McCheyne]. Edinburgh: John Johnstone, 1848.

Finney, C. G. *Lectures on Revivals of Religion*. London: Milner, 1838.

———. *The Prayer-Meeting That Prevailed: A Voice from the '59 Revival*. Edinburgh: "Bright Words" Offices, 1931. First published 1859.

Gillies, John. *Historical Collections of Accounts of Revival*. Edinburgh: Banner of Truth Trust, 1981. First published 1754; revised and enlarged 1845.

*History of St. Peter's Free Church, Dundee*. Dundee, Scotland: Alex. Ewan, 1886.

Hope, John. *A Letter to the Lord Chancellor, on the Claims of the Church of Scotland in regard to its jurisdiction, and on the Proposed Changes in its Polity*. Edinburgh: Wm. Whyte and Co., 1839.

Kyd, James Grey, ed. *Scottish Population Statistics, Including Webster's Analysis of Population, 1755*. Publications of the Scottish History Society, 3rd series, vol. 44. Edinburgh: T. & A. Constable, 1952.

Lamb, William. *McCheyne from the Pew: Being extracts from the diary of William Lamb*. Edited by Kirkwood Hewat. Stirling, Scotland: Drummond's Tract Depot, 1897.

Lewis, George. *The Church in the Fire, and out of the Fire*. Dundee, Scotland: William Middleton, 1841.

————. *The Filth and Fever Bills of Dundee, and what might be made of them*. Dundee, Scotland: William Middleton, 1841.

————. *The Pauper Bill of Dundee, and what should be done with it*. Dundee, Scotland: William Middleton, 1841.

————. *The School Bill of Dundee, and how little can be made of it*. Dundee, Scotland: William Middleton, 1841.

————. *The State of St. David's Parish, with remarks on the Moral and Physical Statistics of Dundee*. Dundee, Scotland: William Middleton, 1841.

————. *The Tavern Bill of Dundee, and what might be made of it*. Dundee, Scotland: William Middleton, 1841.

*List of ministers who adhered to the Resolutions of the Convocation of Edinburgh, 22 November 1842*. Edinburgh: Peter Brown, 1843.

Macfarlan, Duncan. *The Revivals of the Eighteenth Century, particularly at Cambuslang*. London and Edinburgh: John Johnstone, n.d..

McCheyne, R. M. *A Basket of Fragments*. Inverness: Christian Focus, 1979.

———. *The Believer's Joy*. Glasgow: Free Presbyterian, 1987.

———. *Brief Expositions of the Epistles to the Seven Churches of Asia*. Glasgow: N. Adsheed and Son, 1958.

———.*The Eternal Inheritance, the Believer's Portion, and the Vessels of Wrath Fitted to Destruction; Being the Substance of the Two Last Discourses Preached in St. Peter's Church Dundee, Sabbath, March 12, 1843*. Dundee, Scotland: William Middleton, 1843.

———. *From the Preacher's Heart: Sermons and Lectures of Robert Murray McCheyne*. Fearn, Scotland: Christian Focus, 2001.

———. *Letters to Inquirers and Young Converts*. Edinburgh: William Oliphant, 1875.

———. *New Testament Sermons*. Edited by Michael McMullen. Edinburgh: Banner of Truth Trust, 2004.

———. *Old Testament Sermons*. Edited by Michael McMullen. Edinburgh: Banner of Truth Trust, 2004.

———. *The Passionate Preacher: Sermons of Robert Murray McCheyne*. Edited by Michael McMullen. Fearn, Scotland: Christian Focus, 1999.

———. *Sermons on Hebrews*. Edited by Michael McMullen. Edinburgh: Banner of Truth Trust, 2004.

Myles, James. *Chapters in the Life of a Dundee Factory Boy: An Autobiography*. Dundee, Scotland: McCosh, Park and Dewars, 1850.

Ogilvy, Graham, ed. *Dundee: A Voyage of Discovery*. Edinburgh: Mainstream, 1999.

Pike, E. Royston. *Human Documents of the Industrial Revolution in Britain*. London: Allen and Unwin, 1966.

Reid, William. *Authentic Records of Revival now in progress in the United Kingdom*. London: James Nisbet, 1860. Reprint, Wheaton, Ill.: Robert Owen Roberts, 1980.

*Report of the Great Anti-Corn Law meeting held at Dundee, on Thursday, 6th January 1842*. Dundee, Scotland: J. Chalmers, Wm. Livingstone, and F. Shaw, 1842.

*Report of the Presbyterial Committee on Church Extension.* Dundee, Scotland: Chronicle Office, 1837.

*Report of the Proceedings at the Meetings of Members and Friends of the Church of Scotland, in opposition to absolute Patronage and Violent settlements, and in defence of the spiritual independence of the church, 28th and 29th January, 1840.* Dundee, Scotland: William Middleton, 1840.

*Report of the Speeches delivered at the Anti-Endowment Meeting, held in George's Chapel, Dundee, 27th December, 1838.* Dundee, Scotland: Advertiser Office, 1839.

*Report on the Pauperism of Dundee; by a committee appointed at a meeting of the magistrates, heritors and general session.* Dundee, Scotland: David Hill, at the Courier Office, 1839.

*The Revival of Religion: Addresses by Scottish Evangelical Leaders Delivered in Glasgow in 1840.* Edinburgh: Banner of Truth Trust, 1984.

Robe, James. *When the Wind Blows: The Kilsyth and Cambuslang Revivals Factually Recorded.* Kilsyth, Scotland: Ambassador Productions, 1985.

Sprague, William B. *Lectures on Revivals of Religion.* Edinburgh: Banner of Truth Trust, 1978.

*Statement respecting the Non-Intrusion Principle of the Church of Scotland and the modes of its Legislative Recognition by the Non-Intrusion Committee.* Appointed by the General Assembly of the Church.

Willison, John. *The Afflicted Man's Companion.* London and Edinburgh: Nelson, 1899.

———. *A Catechism on the Nature and Uses of the Lord's Supper.* Edinburgh: William Whyte, 1842.

———. *The Mother's Catechism for a Young Child.* Glasgow: John S. Marr & Sons, n.d.

———. *The Young Communicant's Catechism: or a Help, both short and plain, for instructing and preparing the young, to make a right approach to the Lord's Table.* Kilmarnock, Scotland: H. Crawford, 1813.

## Secondary Sources

Arnot, William. *Life of James Hamilton*. 2nd ed. London: James Nisbet, 1870.

Baker, Ernest. *The Revivals of the Bible*. London: Kingsgate Press, 1906.

Beaty, David P. *An All-Surpassing Fellowship: Learning from Robert Murray M'Cheyne's Communion with God*. Grand Rapids: Reformation Heritage Books, 2014.

*Bibliography of Dundee Periodical Literature*, compiled by Alexander C. Lamb. Local History Library, Dundee.

Black, Aileen. *Gilfillan of Dundee 1813–1878: Interpreting Religion and Culture in Mid-Victorian Scotland*. Dundee, Scotland: Dundee University Press, 2006.

Blaikie, W. G. *The Preachers of Scotland from the Sixth to the Nineteenth Century*. Edinburgh: Banner of Truth Trust, 2001.

Bonar, Horatius. *Life of the Rev. John Milne of Perth*. 4th ed. London: James Nisbet, 1868.

Bonar, Marjory, ed. *Reminiscences of Andrew Bonar*. London: Hodder and Stoughton, 1877.

Bowles, John. *The Autobiography or History of the Life of John Bowles*. Glasgow: G. Gallie & Son; Dundee: McGregor and Wise, 1872.

Brown, Callum G. *Religion and Society in Scotland since 1707*. Edinburgh: Edinburgh University Press, 1997.

Brown, S. J. "The Disruption and Urban Poverty: Thomas Chalmers and the West Port Operation in Edinburgh, 1844–47." *Records of the Scottish Church History Society* 20 (1978): 65–89.

———. *Thomas Chalmers and the Godly Commonwealth*. Oxford: Oxford University Press, 1982.

Brown, S. J., and Michael Fry, eds. *Scotland in the Age of Disruption*. Edinburgh: Edinburgh University Press, 1993.

Brown, Thomas. *Annals of the Disruption*. Edinburgh: Macniven and Wallace, 1893.

Burleigh, J. H. S. *A Church History of Scotland*. Oxford: Oxford University Press, 1960.

Burns, James. *Revivals and Their Leaders*. London: Hodder and Stoughton, 1909.

Cameron, Nigel M. De S., ed. *Dictionary of Scottish Church History and Theology*. Edinburgh: T&T Clark, 1993.

Cook, Paul E. G. *Revival in History*. Located in the Evangelical Library, London.

Couper, W. J. et al. *Scotland Saw His Glory: A History of Revivals in Scotland*. Edited by Richard Owen Roberts. Wheaton, Ill.: International Awakening Press, 1955.

Currie, D. A. "The Growth of Evangelicalism in the Church of Scotland, 1793–1843." PhD diss., St. Andrews University, 1991.

Douglas, J. D., ed. *The New International Dictionary of the Christian Church*. Exeter: Paternoster Press, 1974.

Drummond, A. L., and James Bulloch. *The Church in Victorian Scotland, 1843–1874*. Edinburgh: St. Andrews Press, 1975.

———. *The Scottish Church 1688–1843*. Edinburgh: St. Andrews Press, 1981.

Fawcett, Arthur. *The Cambuslang Revival: The Scottish Evangelical Revival of the Eighteenth Century*. Edinburgh: Banner of Truth Trust, 1996.

Gauldie, Enid. *Cruel Habitations: A History of Working-Class Housing, 1780–1918*. London: Allan & Unwin, 1974.

———. "The Middle Class and Working-Class Housing in the Nineteenth Century." In *Social Class in Scotland: Past and Present*, ed. A. Allan Maclaren, 12–35. Edinburgh: John Donald, 1976.

Haslam, David F. "Robert Murray M'Cheyne (1813–1843)." The Robert Murray M'Cheyne Resource. http://www.mcheyne.info/.

Hayden, Eric W. *Spurgeon on Revival*. Grand Rapids: Zondervan, 1962.

Inglis, Andrew. *Notes of the History of Dudhope Free Church, Lochee Road, Dundee*. Dundee, Scotland: James P. Mathew, 1890.

Kennedy, John. *The Apostle of the North: The Life and Labours of the Rev. John MacDonald, DD of Ferintosh*. Glasgow: Free Presbyterian Publications, 1978.